BLACK AND WHITE STRIKE GOLD

Practical Nuggets to Grow Your Business from the Women Who Launched Consultants 2 Go, a Multi-Million Dollar Company

By Sandi Webster and Peggy McHale

BLACK AND WHITE STRIKE GOLD
Practical Nuggets to Grow Your Business from the Women Who Launched
Consultants 2 Go, a Multi-Million Dollar Company

ISBN 13: 978-0-9842786-0-2

C2G Publishing
105 Lock Street, Suite 309
Newark, NJ 07103

Printed in the USA.

Acknowledgments

We would like to thank our families, the Consultants 2 Go (C2G) team, especially Annette Giordano, and friends for the support and encouragement they have shown us during this process. We truly appreciate all the feedback that you gave us.

A big *Thank You* to our Board of Advisors and the Count Me In team for the Make Mine a Million $ Business program. Libby Ladu, you always gave us great advice, especially around structuring the publishing division, and Nell Merlino gave us inspiration.

Bonnie St. John, thanks for introducing us to Sophfronia Scott, our great editor, and much thanks to Julie Trelstad at Plain White Press.

Peggy: Thanks to my mother, Beatrice Engels, who taught me to stand on my own two feet; my husband, Robert McHale who gave me lots of common sense advice and practical sales tips from the beginning; and Rob McHale Jr., who was enthusiastic from the start and came up with our original tagline for the company. Emily McHale gets a special shout out for reading the rough draft and making editing comments.

Sandi: Thanks to my mother, Valda Webster, for always, always supporting me in whatever I chose to do, and to Larry McCord for giving me fantastic "how-to-proceed" information.

And to the cast of C2G characters and consultants: We could not have done it without you.

Contents

Contents

Foreword

By Nell Merlino

It's my belief that the successful women of the world don't wait for the world to change in their favor. They change it themselves. They create the work they want, the relationships they want, the life they want. The results are brilliantly apparent. Sandi and Peggy are two such women. When I met them in 2006 they had already started their consulting company and that year brought in $350,000 in revenue. That alone would have been enough for most women. But they knew they were building something so much more. They were interested in the Make Mine a Million $ Business program and the tools and mentoring it offered to women-owned businesses.

Sandi entered the Make Mine a Million $ Business contest and, not surprisingly considering her and Peggy's great focus, won a place as one of the 20 finalists in New York. They aggressively utilized all the tools of the program and, by December 2006, their company had hurdled over the million-dollar mark. Here's the great thing about what they accomplished: Sandi and Peggy knew what they wanted and sought the tools and assistance they needed to get them there. It's an example anyone would do well to model.

Now they've written this wonderful book to help you do just that. This book tells their journey from start-up to success story. You'll get to share in all the learnings they have had in every situation, including the current economic downturn. In each chapter you'll find excellent examples of what good businesswomen should and should not do. Their advice is easy to understand and to execute. I know that sometimes it helps to see how someone else did something before figuring out if you can do it yourself.

As they say, success leaves clues. But it's not always easy to find such clues because not all successful businesspeople are willing to share their secrets. Sandi and Peggy's willingness to open the book on both their triumphs and their failures is a testament to the strength of their characters and their purpose. They know that the best way for more women to have million-dollar businesses is for those who have already achieved it to shine a light on the path. I wish them all the best with this new opportunity to bring their advice – and their light – to the world.

Introduction

In 2002, Consultants 2 Go was born. It was the "child" of Sandra (Sandi) Webster and Marguerite (Peggy) McHale, two colleagues from American Express who lost their jobs after the terrorist attacks of September 11th. Sandi and Peggy are of different races (Sandi's black and Peggy's white) and come from very different backgrounds, yet they both shared the same dream to start and build a company. Their unique backgrounds and diverse views helped shape their company.

By 2006, they had already achieved the major accomplishment of growing the company beyond the $1 million mark. Only 3% of all women-owned businesses ever attain this level. The percentage is even smaller for those firms owned by women of different colors. Their success continues in spite of the odds: the firm earned over $2.2 million in revenues in 2008.

How did they do this? What lessons can you learn from them? Read their nuggets of wisdom along with their inspiring stories so that you too can beat the odds and make millions.

How Did We Get Here?

Sandi's Story

The road to entrepreneurship starts early and sometimes ends early. Some entrepreneurs are born and some are born of necessity but the road you walk is the same even though processes may be accelerated.

Born or Learned?

To understand how I wound up in this place where I am, first you have to understand where I'm coming from. So let's do a little word association.

Jamaican-Born = immigrant. That can be a bad word in America, a fact that I don't fully understand because this is a country made up of immigrants. It doesn't matter the age at which you came over on the boat; nor does it matter that you don't know anyone in your native land. What matters is that now and forever, you wear the "immigrant" label even if you become a citizen. Life isn't fair for immigrants. At the end of the day, what the word "immigrant" means to me is that someone in my family is always hustling for the almighty dollar.

Brooklyn-Raised. To middle-America, this connotation is tough, street, ghetto, unmannerly – a lot of words associated with a lot of negatives. As with all myths, it bears some facts, but Brooklyn is what I've known throughout my life and it doesn't hold the same meanings for me. To me, Brooklyn means the greatest diversity of people in, probably, the entire world. At P.S. 233, my school had at least 10 different nationalities – I just knew they were my

1

friends and we shared whatever we brought for lunch. Being from Brooklyn means the ability to adapt to any situation without thinking because it's second nature, i.e., street talk with my friends (from every nation) and "corporate" speak when necessary. I have lived with Hassidics in Flatbush in the '80s and in Crown Heights in the '90s; and in Canarsie in the '70s with the Italians who burned crosses on your lawn, and now in Canarsie in 2009 with African-American and Asian populations who only know the crosses they see at Holy Family church. I have seen entire neighborhoods change in front of me – and you have to adapt or move, which means changing jobs, school and friends. So I have adapted.

African-American. I'm simply Black. I'm not African and frankly, if you go by birth, I'm not American. Jamerican is the term that Jamaicans use to describe people who are Jamaican-born, American-raised. But we are in Brooklyn, and Black in America means ALL black people regardless of nationality or citizenship. To delve a little further, within the Black community, there is definitely a class structure. West Indians are thought to be well-educated service people (doctors in their own country and janitors in the hospitals here). African-Americans call West Indians uppity Negro people who think they're better than their African-American counterparts because they are always trying to buy homes, have nice cars and send their children to schools in white neighborhoods. The uppity Negro myth has some truth, not because West Indians think they are better but because our parents are forceful in their want of better for their children. It's the typical immigrant mentality that this is the land where dreams become reality. I took flack from African-American children because they said my parents were trying to take their parents' jobs, and I took flack from White kids for being Black. Basically, I learned to fight – and win – at a very early age.

Female. We carry the burden of our families. We are responsible for the home, including contributing to the household income regardless of our age. As a female child, I cooked, cleaned and shopped while my mother worked her two to three jobs to keep a roof over our heads. My brother didn't do "girl" chores; his "job" was to go to Columbia University – and he did – and to help the family later in life. My sister is five years younger than I am, so I learned how to take care of children. As a female adult, I learned that no matter how hard I worked, I would get paid less than a barely-working man; that after taxes, what I netted would be equivalent to the money I would have earned if I stayed at home and cooked, cleaned and shopped while my spouse worked two to three jobs to take care of me.

And so this background laid the foundation for some of my first entrepreneurial ventures: turning on lights for Jewish people on Friday evenings for $1; being a home attendant on weekends to a 90+-year-old man – a teenager could get paid for just sitting there and talking to him. Crocheting was a very real business, and there was money to be made in handmade garments, so I crocheted. And last but not least, there was babysitting. In the '70s, babysitting was always one of the first jobs that a young person could get, and I got a lot. By the time I was 15, I went from babysitting to running a nursery school out of the basement and garage.

I learned that it was impossible to like and please everyone, but you still had to do the work…and I liked the money, of which there was plenty. I learned that it's difficult to get respect from older people when a younger person is either telling them what to do or taking care of their child better than they can. As a matter of fact, at that time, it was frustrating to be young. I learned that if you don't know something, ask somebody who knows; they'll be happy to share information with you and steer you on the right path (get a mentor). Most important, it taught me that I can control my own destiny by producing my own income. If I had stayed in childcare, I would have been a millionaire many times over.

Basically, I learned how to be an entrepreneur because that is what my environment taught me.

Planting Seeds

The parents of the children in my daycare were getting restless. They started to purposefully find faults every day so they wouldn't have to pay me. I was

17, and the childcare laws were changing and becoming regulated, so I would need to get licensed and all kinds of new-fangled stuff that would make my life hell. My mother, the unionized-for-life, democratic factory worker, wanted me to get a real job. She wondered why she was working several jobs to send me to school and there I was, babysitting? "Go get a real job," she said. So I started to work at the NYC Board of Education while going to Erasmus Hall Performing Arts High School. It was one of my good fortunes to have started out at the very beginning of a great program, Title I Children's Program: Learning to Read Through the Arts. It was headed up by a woman! Bernadette O'Brien was trying to get funding for a new program she was putting together. This program was teaching children who had a problem reading and writing how to use the arts to communicate more effectively, and it was perfect because I was a theater and dance major. Grant proposals had to be written. Class curriculum had to be put together. And I did it with very little instruction and continued doing it for years while going to Brooklyn College and studying theater and dance. Having that major helped tremendously with my work on arts program curricula, but at the end of the day, I was still a minimum wage-paid, valuable asset. I needed to make more money, so I left the Board of Education.

My cousin Cynthia worked at Saks Fifth Avenue and immediately found me an administrative slot that was paying almost twice the salary of my Board of Ed job. I typed over 120 words per minute on a manual typewriter, so it was an easy job for me responding to presidential complaints from phenomenally wealthy women who wasted postage to request finance charge refunds of a penny. I worked 9 years at Saks, moving through different positions. I learned customer service, collections, capital expenditure, catalog marketing and information management. I made good friends, and I still maintain most of those close relationships today.

Around that time I changed schools from Brooklyn College where I was a theater major, to Baruch (an accounting school) in the evening program as it was closer to my job. I took one or two classes per semester – that's all the time that I had. Then I hit a snag. There was a required class that I needed to take for my degree but they didn't teach the class at night. I switched to NYU to take the class – it was on database marketing and segmentation. I was good at it. At my day job, I was working at Saks in the database marketing department. Unknown to me at the time, this class would be instrumental in my future.

My boss, James, left Saks and went to American Express (Amex.) He said financial services paid more money than retail and I should consider it. I did, and James got me a job as the secretary to the VP of database marketing. I made a deal with the VP that after one year I would find my own replacement and take the first lower level management position that came along. Exactly a year later, I became an account rep in the customer information management department and worked another 15 years at Amex.

During my 16 years, I did database marketing, process reengineering and trained incoming new hires on marketing on the consumer side of the business before moving to the actual marketing department on the business side. That's where I met my current business partner, Peggy. She was my new boss and started a few days after I got to that department. We would speak about our dreams of owning our own company. Three years later, we really bonded over a difficult project that I headed up for our department. That experience helped me make the decision to leave Amex so I could take charge of my life. I had already begun planning my exit within the next two years by buying property in Pennsylvania. I planned to rent out these houses and have it become my second income. I was on House #1.

September 11th changed all that. On that fateful day, as I stood at the bus stop waiting for my express bus from Canarsie, I changed my mind and walked back around the corner to the school across from my house to cast my vote in the New York City primaries. I always waited until the last minute to run home and catch the polls and figured I might as well do it now. I would be a few minutes late to the office, but since I spent upwards of 16 hours there, it really didn't matter if I was MIA for a few minutes. I missed

5

my bus. Missing that bus probably saved my life. I would have been walking through the World Trade Center at the exact time that the planes hit. Because of my delay, I was watching history unfold from the window of a bus on the Gowanus Expressway.

I wasn't sure what was going on in the World Trade, but I knew something was going on because I remembered the bombing in '93 – I thought one of those helicopters had finally lost control and went through a window. As I saw smoke streaming from the tower, I screamed for our bus driver not to go through the Battery Tunnel or we would be stuck there for the day. Our bus driver was new to the job and insisted that he could not change his route. There were a few people on my bus who were there in '93 and started screaming with me. Somehow, we got through to him because he made a sharp, illegal U-turn right before he entered the tunnel. His decision saved us a lot of grief that day. We watched as flames started coming out of the second tower, and we knew that it was more than a simple mistake. We knew a lot of people in those towers.

When I got home, my mother was outside crying with my neighbors because she thought I had caught my original bus. They were all shocked and happy to see me. My mother hugged and kissed me. I asked what happened and that's when I found out that two airplanes had intentionally flown into the World Trade Center towers.

After that day, I worked from home because the American Express building was right across the street from the World Trade Center and was also damaged. My team moved to the old AT&T building in Short Hills, NJ. I knew layoffs would happen, and I was actually looking forward to it. I knew I would take whatever package was offered to me regardless of how secure I wanted to feel. September 11th had given me my wings to fly. I was no longer satisfied with my job. It was time to move on.

I was one of the chosen few who got laid off. Peggy was another. It was my first time ever being let go from any job. I received a severance package. I took it and danced around the floor. In hindsight, I probably should have been a little lower key with my joy! Most people said I was one of the happiest laid-off people they had ever seen. Our senior management wanted me to stay and take over another fledgling department, growing a business that consisted mainly of funeral homes, but I declined. I was happy to be alive. I was happy to start phase two of my life. I was happy to leave the craziness of corporate life behind…and I was happy to start speaking to Peggy about getting out of Dodge.

How Did We Get Here?

Peggy's Story

Ever since I can remember, I always wanted to have my own business. Other little girls I knew wanted to grow up and get married and have children, but not me. I dreamed about owning a large company with many divisions. In fact, by the time I was eight, I already had named the company, "Peggy's Posies." But this wasn't going to be one ordinary little shop – No! I envisioned an empire that would be larger than FTD. I would have a worldwide network of stores that would bear this brand name. Little did I know that I was actually imagining 1-800-FLOWERS.

So how did I get to be 43 and working at American Express without realizing the dream? Remember the little girl with the big idea? Well it all started there. While she had the big dream, she didn't always have the self-confidence that she could really do it.

The Beginning…

My mom was ahead of her time in many of her views. She told me to never trust men and always be independent. And for my mom, that meant financial independence. She told me that I must always work and be self-sufficient. Never, ever rely on anyone to support you…no matter what. In fact, I could write a separate book on the events in her life that drove her to these views. My mother was also a big proponent of education. She wanted all three of her children to get a college education, something she chose not to pursue even though she had a four-year scholarship to Hunter College. She decided to get married and gave up her scholarship, a decision she regretted her entire life. In fact, I can never remember my mom being truly happy until she started down the path to entrepreneurship. She became a real estate broker in the early 1970s and ultimately opened her own office. It was during those decades when she ran her own business and wasn't dependent on my father for money, that she seemed the happiest. She always lamented marrying my father and giving up her education. Then out of guilt, she would always add that she was glad that she had her children. I know she truly loved us, but she never got over the things that happened in her life and as her youngest child and only daughter, she continually reinforced these feelings with me.

My Irish Catholic parents were products of the Great Depression. To them, particularly my mother, a steady job with a steady income was one of the best things you could accomplish in your life. My father, the eldest of nine boys and son of a troubled father, often had "pie in the sky" dreams for quick wealth and success. I think this came from his impoverished childhood where he would fantasize about becoming a star or some other type of success so that he could save his family. He had to work at 14 to put food on the table since his own father lost his job in 1932 and did not go back to work until 1941.

As a result of his upbringing, my father had a fierce temper, and my brothers were often afraid of him. I never was! He loved us all, but he never got over his poverty-ridden childhood, and he could be very erratic. This made living with him very difficult at times. My eldest brother Jimmy bore the brunt of this relationship and paid for it the rest of his life. My brother Eddy and I witnessed some of this tension when we were growing up, and I think it made us closer as a result. Ed was only two years older than me and was "naturally" smart. My mother and father would always comment that his high IQ was just like my mother's. In fact, in later years if Eddy said something, it had to be true – at least according to Mom. Fortunately for C2G, Ed was a CPA, and he ultimately agreed to be our company's accountant and helped us with forming the company.

I was the "different one" of the three kids. My mom said I was the one born with common sense and a competitive spirit. I was a good student with a drive to always push forward. As a result, when I graduated from the College of Mount Saint Vincent, I was recruited and hired by New York Telephone into their management-training program. My family was very proud of me, and my grandmother even commented that I had a job for life. This was a little frightening for me but I never shared those feelings with anyone. In my family's eyes, I really was beginning to live the American Dream. I had this "great job" with an excellent salary so who would ever consider doing anything different? Then shortly after my career began, I met the man who became my husband, and we started to save for a house. Practically speaking, the idea of starting my own business would have been thought of as foolhardy by everyone. Why would you give up all this for a very uncertain future? In fact, the message was, "Don't take the risk. Don't fail."

I made other risk-averse decisions in my career as well. One of my favorite bosses and mentors, Jack, wanted me to apply for the Executive MBA program at Columbia. This would have been a great opportunity for me, but I didn't do it. Instead I made excuses and said I would go to school at night. I wound up getting my MBA from St. John's University. A good school but certainly not the same caliber as Columbia. Why didn't I pursue Columbia? Because I thought I wouldn't get in, and I was afraid to fail. I didn't think I was smart enough. In fact, I repeated this behavior many times in my life. I wouldn't attempt something because at heart, I didn't believe I could do it and being a perfectionist, I didn't want to fail. It was only later in my life that I began to realize that failures are great teachers. Sometimes it is through our failures that we learn more about things and, most important, about ourselves.

I spent 17 years at AT&T (which is where I wound up after the split of the Bell System in 1984). As I moved up in the ranks, there were some detours to have my two wonderful children. I began to realize that maybe I wasn't quite as average as I thought. I also noticed that I was a very quick study and enjoyed those positions that let me do something new. AT&T was also where I really found an area in corporate life that I really liked – marketing. Eventually, I was able to muster the courage to leave when we were offered a great voluntary buy-out package in 1998. My husband was very nervous about my decision since he too came from a family that weathered the depression and valued a steady job as the means to prosperity. So while I got to leave AT&T, I knew I had to get another job quickly.

Staying home full-time was never an option for me. I had worked part-time at AT&T for four years so that I could better balance family and work, but I realized that for many reasons (including that little voice of my mother's) I enjoyed the outside stimulation of a job and the lifestyle it afforded us. More important, I liked the independence of having my own paycheck and assets!

I believe it was the decision to leave AT&T that was my first step towards entrepreneurship. I decided I wanted to work for a smaller company, to see if I would really like that environment. My one year at Paragon, an IT consulting firm, was a tremendous experience. I never worked so hard and learned so much in such a compressed amount of time. I realized when I left Paragon that I loved working for a small company. But next time, I thought, it would have to be mine. However, I also realized that when you outgrow a small company, unlike a large one, there is no other place to go within that company. I left Paragon to go to American Express as a vice president. I had considered joining a small start-up as a minority owner but felt their business model was not quite right. So I made a strategic move to increase my contacts, move to the next level and learn a new industry. I always knew that I wasn't going to stay to get the "gold watch" but to use the experience to help me be successful with the company I would start. How right and wrong I was with this move.

The Catalyst

It was a crystal clear blue sky that day. In fact, as I sat on the ferry, I breathed deeply and inhaled the crisp air and realized it held a slight hint of fall that morning. I skimmed the free Daily News that was given to me as I entered the ferry and looked at pictures of an emaciated Whitney Houston.

I asked myself again if I could hold on for a few more years before I would start the company. I really pined for my kids because the commute and the long hours kept me away from home much of the week. Every day, I would ask myself if I had made the right decision. I had worked yet again, another 80-hour week, so my boss could present our 2002 plan to the company President. I was doing this on a consistent basis for two years and staying late almost every night. I even dropped things off at her house on weekends so we could continue to refine our presentation. The hours were horrendous and I wasn't sure if the sacrifice was really worth it. In fact, I thought about my discussion with Sandi the prior month, where I shared my dreams about starting a business. We had really connected over the summer when she was working on a very difficult assignment and planning a company outing as well. I told her that I knew that American Express was a great place to work and it would provide a tremendous network for a business, but the toll on my personal life was beginning to make me rethink my strategy. She acknowledged that she was rethinking her plans too.

As I stepped off the ferry and walked the short block to my office. I went to the cafeteria and got my usual Starbucks. When I paid the lady at the register, I noticed a commotion. Some of the workers started running towards the windows and said there was a fire at the World Trade Center. I went over to look and expected to see some smoke. When I looked up and saw the large gaping hole spewing flames and smoke, I realized this was no ordinary fire. I thought, "Should I turn around and go or take the elevator and get my laptop?" Just then the PA system came on: "Please feel safe and return to your offices. The fire is contained to the other building, and it is safe to go upstairs." I still didn't realize that a plane had flown into the building, so I headed to the elevators and up to my office on the 34th floor. Another man on the elevator mentioned that a plane hit the World Trade Center. I asked, "One of those little ones?" and he replied, "No, a jet." "Wow that's surprising! Aren't pilots trained to ditch it rather than hit a building?" He just shook his head as I walked off the elevator. I opened my office door and noticed all three lines were ringing. I grabbed the first one and it was my sister-in-law, June. She told me that an airplane had hit the Trade Center. Then my husband, Robert, and my mother called. As I was talking to them, the second plane hit the South Tower. With that, I told them that I would leave and call when I was on my way home.

I went down the 34 flights of stairs and onto Vesey Street which ran parallel to the Towers. There was debris flying, and firemen, EMTs and policemen were running up towards the buildings. Sirens were blaring, and people were everywhere. I quickly decided that the ferries were the best way home that day. I went over to the terminal, and there were hundreds of people in line to leave. We all stared back up at the building transfixed by the sights. I tried to call my family from my cell phone but the circuits were all busy.

I took the first available ferry that arrived at the dock and left. As I got to the other side, the first tower began to crumble. People stood in the streets not believing what they were seeing. People wept and hugged complete strangers. I was frantic because I knew my family was worried and I needed to reach them. I met a really nice man from Oppenheimer who told me I could use his phone in his apartment house. Eventually, I got through and let everyone know that I was OK. I waited on line for a bus to Newark and finally got there by 3 p.m. My husband picked me up, and we both embraced, knowing that I was lucky to get out alive.

The next days and weeks were a haze. We could not return to the American Express building since it was severely damaged. American Express placed us at temporary quarters in New Jersey. Then in mid-October, the company decided to do a massive layoff since they were so negatively impacted by 9/11. Sandi and I both were given notice on the same day by our boss. While I was pretty shaken up about the lay off, I knew I could never go back to another corporate job. Fortunately, we each received a generous severance package from the company and within a week, we started collaborating on potential business ventures; and that's when we began to form our business, Consultants 2 Go.

The Start of Something Big: C2G – The Book

We both took some well-needed time off. Sandi trekked around South Africa while I joyfully chauffeured my children to school. Sandi painted every room in her house, fixed up the yard and washed every dish in the cabinet until there was nothing left to do. I became a soccer mom, and it was all about the kids. Then enough was enough. We decided it was time to get down to business. We were people used to multi-tasking, and we wanted to take the same time and care in building this business. We made a conscious decision to invest in our business for at least a year to see where it would take us and learn from the mistakes that were made along the way.

Since we started the business, we have been unwittingly collecting information for this book. Each day held some kind of amazement for us. We were surprised at some of the things people did for us, without solicitation, and strictly with the intention of helping us. We were shocked at the people who tried to rip us off because we were women, because they thought they could get away with it, or just because they were sleazy individuals.

"Well, this will go into a chapter of our book!" It was a joke between us when something unbelievable happened to us. But more and more, as we built the business, we were asked to speak at events or to give advice to other small business owners or individuals who were thinking of starting a business. Writing this book creates several check marks for us. First, it is a consolidation of events that occurred while growing our business over the $1 million threshold. Most of the names and situations have been changed. Second, we decided to gather all the advice that people have been asking of us. We wanted an organized method of disbursing the information.

We hope your takeaway from this book is to understand some of the obstacles that arose in our journey and how we handled the situations. You do not have to agree with us, but we ask that you keep an open mind.

We feel women will gain more from our advice as the camaraderie among women is phenomenal. Not to say that men won't gain any insights, but this book is being written from the perspective of two women and, therefore, women might relate and identify with us a lot faster.

This book is a quick, easy read. Our tips are really nuggets of learning more so than advice. Some of it we also read in other books but didn't quite get it until we had experienced it ourselves– you probably won't get it at first either, but we want to reinforce it all. Other nuggets are things that could only happen to us! We took turns writing chapters and then giving our version of what the other person wrote. It's not in chronological order but more in order of what we think is important. We hope you can see the contrast in our thinking as well as where we sync up on particular ideas. Despite our different backgrounds and ethnicities, our thinking is more similar than you might guess. Unfortunately, this may reinforce the idea that Sandi and Peggy are the same person (Pandi, as we are affectionately called by some of our clients).

Thank you for participating in our continued adventure.

NUGGET #1 **Believe in You!**

By Peggy

This sounds like a cliché, but this chapter is where the dream of your business begins and belief in yourself is essential for success. *No one will ever support your dream if you don't.* Once you start down the road to entrepreneurship, write down your vision for the business. Commit it to memory and repeat it to yourself. Tell yourself that you can do it and surround yourself with people who will support you in the pursuit of your dream. *You really have to believe in you to make it happen.*

Starting a business is one of the biggest leaps of faith you will take. Be sure that you are absolutely committed to your success. When Sandi and I started down this path, we always believed we would be successful. We had a dream that we would create a multi-million dollar consulting firm. While there have been many tough days in the seven years we have been in business, this belief kept us going even during the most difficult times and powered us with the sense that we could accomplish anything.

Our advice to anyone considering this path is to map out the vision and also understand the obstacles that might get in the way of your belief that you can achieve this kind of success. You need to feel really secure about yourself and who you are. *If you have doubts, check them at the door. You must push on in spite of the obstacles you will encounter. Make sure you have a support group that reinforces the "you can do it" message; otherwise, you can get very down, and your self-confidence will erode.*

I think this has been one of the reasons we were able to get here – we both knew our strengths and weaknesses, and you must know the same. Be very honest with yourself – check your gut on this one – this is not the time to practice self-deception. If you know that you are good at some tasks like selling or operations, do them. But if you are horrible with money or paperwork, outsource them to a bookkeeper or a virtual assistant. In our case, since we had a partnership, we were able to divvy up the tasks between us, putting our unique talents to work. Again, this wouldn't have worked unless we were brutally honest about strengths and weaknesses upfront.

It is also important to know who you need to be around – a critical success factor for any wanna-be entrepreneur. All of us know people who are our cheerleaders. Go to them for the advice and support that reinforces the "You can do it" message. *But be aware of the negative people* – they will stomp on your dream and create doubt in your mind. I have a colleague who was not supportive at all. He was extremely negative about the business and my ability to be successful; I realized pretty quickly that I needed to distance myself from him when it came to the business, since he was sapping all of my positive energy. We are still friends, but I don't discuss my business with him because it would be counterproductive – and he doesn't ask.

And remember everyone – clients, colleagues and employees – all feel the vibe you give off. If you believe in what you can do, they will believe in you as well. That doesn't mean you don't admit when you don't know something. But if you have doubts, they will also sense it and hold back, thus reducing your chances of achieving your dreams.

Sandi: Peggy is correct. My mother and grandmother always told me that I could do whatever I wanted to do. I always believed in myself. I come from a family of ridiculously strong women who passed, and continue to pass, that message of belief on to other female family members. Not many people have that foundation of strength, especially women.

I've always been very analytical about what I want to do. This nature helps to support my self-belief system. Even before I was formally told in classes and books that I read (and by Oprah) that I had to write down my vision, I always wrote notes to myself because when I see it, I believe it. I reinforce this message to myself twice a year, on my birthday and on New Year's Day. I write down my personal goals for the New Year and at the end of the year, since my birthday is in November, I stop and take a look at what I've done to accomplish those goals. I ask myself, "Did you believe you could do this?" When I see things in writing, it helps me to be realistic. *I do the easy things first so it gives me positive feedback in believing what I can do.* Who wants a bunch of impossible tasks?

When I turned 35, I opened up my birthday to all my friends. At my all-girl "parties," I select a life topic for us to discuss and spend a few hours talking about our dreams and supporting each other. It is my way of forming a support group for me and my friends. (2008's topic was Our Bucket Lists!) Do I believe I can do all those 47 things or visit those places on my list before I kick it? I will die trying! Remarkably, I have done at least ten things on that list.

Pick a time that you consistently write down your goals and check up on your vision. After a few successes…and a few learnings…you too will believe in yourself by seeing what is possible.

NUGGET #2 **Follow Your Passion!**

By Peggy

Passion will fuel your dreams. *You need to create a business that you will enjoy and have fun owning.* This is connected to Nugget #1 – Believe in You. How can you possibly be successful if you don't like what you do nor have fun creating it?

As long as I can remember, my dream and passion was to have my own business. Remember that little girl? Well, she finally got that chance in 2002. I enjoyed marketing, but for me, the fun was in creating something new and running it. Consultants 2 Go gave me the chance to combine my love of marketing with my passion for entrepreneurship.

How did I decide that a consulting company was something I could get "charged up" about? It wasn't an intellectual decision for me; it was from the "gut." I didn't dream of a consulting business, but through my life experiences, I knew this was the right thing to do when I left American Express. Through self-examination and my work experiences, I realized that for me, the thrill was in starting a business and having it succeed. While I still enjoyed flowers and the thought of Peggy's Posies, my real desire was to leverage my years of experience so that I would be in a better position to achieve my goal. The hard part was convincing people that we really wanted to make consulting a business. Many people say they are consulting when they are unemployed so it had become something of a stigma. However, I was so passionate about it that I doodled ideas on napkins, thought about it during my fitness walks and dreamed about it in the middle of the night!

Sandi, my business partner, has a real passion for working with young adults. While our core clients are Fortune 500 businesses, she is still able to channel this desire by speaking to high school groups about our business and sharing with them the abundant opportunities that come with owning your own business. This desire to serve as a role model, particularly to teens who might come from economically disadvantaged homes, helps drive her and us to greater success.

Now you are probably saying to yourself, "That's great, but I don't have a clue as to what makes me happy." Think about the things you enjoy doing, whether it's a specific activity at work, a hobby or something you do as a volunteer. Or maybe you are like me; I just knew I had to own my own business. It took me twenty years to figure out what type of business. After I left AT&T, I went to work for a smaller consulting firm. That's when I realized that consulting was what I was meant to do. It didn't happen overnight but it gave me practical insight on how to get started and what it would take. By working for Paragon, I began to see the possibilities and when I left there, I knew I liked working for a small company. I also realized that the next small company I would work for would be mine.

Sandi: I remember when we fleshed out our basic idea of what this business would be. I say basic because our ideas continue to change depending on the economy and the business need. Both Peggy and I were part of a program at Drake Beam, the outplacement firm that American Express gave us as part of our severance package. We were in different centers – me in New York and Peg in New Jersey. When I presented the business idea to my counselor, Maxine, she said she felt how passionate I was about making this work. I knew I had communicated that passion because she got on board our C2G train by helping me with picking the logo and color for the company. She became just as excited as we were. Maxine and I are still in touch, and recently she asked me to speak at her meeting of newly unemployed people because she wants C2G to be an inspiration to them and for me to convey the passion that we still have for starting and running our own company.

Nugget #2 Follow Your Passion!

When we presented our business idea later at a different Drake Beam open forum that included men, we were clear that we wanted to grow to $2 million within three to five years. I don't recall who said it but distinctly recall a man saying that was not possible and was just a pipe dream. We were so passionate about what we wanted to do that we questioned why he thought it couldn't work – and he couldn't concretely tell us. We listened to him but ignored him – he was just an outlier in our dreams.

If you are not willing to wake up and work in your business every day, stand in front of Fortune 500 executives to sell them on your vision, or try to share and teach others about what you do; perhaps you are just "in like" with what you want to do, and not necessarily passionate about it. Many people, out of necessity, are not doing the things they are passionate about as their main career, but somehow they find the time to do it as a hobby. Identify what you like to do for fun, and you are closer to identifying your passion.

NUGGET #3 **Enjoy Your Job**

By Sandi

When I entered corporate America, my goal was to make enough money so that I could retire early and go do the things that I actually liked. I did not equate my job with something that I liked to do – it was something that put food on the table. I used to hear old people say, "Do something you really love, and the money will come." I thought that was a joke because, in my mind, when you do something that you love, it's called a hobby. And you never have enough time to work on your hobby.

Then as I got older and went to the career development coaches that were given to corporate executives, I started to realize that the things that brought me success earlier in life were the hobbies that I liked. My babysitting job turned into a day care center; my mindless crocheting that I did to make gifts could be sold to customers who liked handmade items.

So I learned as I progressed through corporate life to look for something that I liked to do. Once that happened, I would automatically work harder, get promoted, and that's when the money came. When I became an expert at what I did, I felt free to share learnings with others. I arrived at work early before anyone else, and I was the last to leave, only to go home, shower, pay the bills and come back again. If someone told me to pack my bags and leave, I would have been devastated, not at the prospect of leaving the company, but mostly because I really liked the work I was doing.

When I was trying to decide what to do with my life after the layoff, I went back to the roots of what I enjoyed. I wanted something that incorporated all my skills and something that I liked enough to work hard at. Now that I am my own boss, I am the only one pushing me to work harder, harder and harder – and I work harder than ever. I know that if I don't like what I do, the sales won't come in…the mortgage won't get paid…the college tuition will stop…and so on.

There are days when I wake up at 6 a.m. and don't move from my computer until midnight. I do this because I enjoy what I do now. Many people tell me that I am a workaholic and that is partially true. But my bottom line is that I don't work like a maniac at things that I don't enjoy – whether it's a finance class (I'll skip it), a networking event (I'll sit in a corner and not speak to anyone), or at a sales pitch (I will realize halfway through that I'm not prepared.) It's different when I'm building a business or a team, creating strategies for other people as well as for myself or working on new projects. Yes, I did that in corporate for good money but it's a different feeling when you have a sense of accomplishment at the end of the day and can't wait to get up tomorrow – all for you. I also know when Peggy is excited and enjoying a new project or idea because she drives me crazy by calling me every five minutes with a new idea.

Peggy: I work longer hours than ever but somehow it feels less like work. While there are days when I say, "Why did I do this? A job would be so much easier," there is so much more satisfaction when you are creating your own business. I am learning so much each day and using all of my skills, so I really have to say this is what I was meant to do. I have never looked back, and the hours fly by. That's how I know I am really enjoying my business!

NUGGET #4 Sink or Swim, But Take the Dive Head First

By Sandi

When I was a little girl, I used to say that I was going to work in a big office in a big company. I would have my own desk, and I would be the boss, simply because I was…well, bossy! One year I went to visit my grandmother in Jamaica, and she asked me what business I was going to own. My grandmother had a 6th grade education and was one of the smartest women I knew. I promptly told her that I was going to be a stewardess (called air hostess back then). Of course, I didn't know I was only going to be five feet tall, and there was a height requirement for that job! My grandmother, who was slightly afraid to fly, countered with saying that if I owned the iron bird (nickname for an airplane), then I wouldn't even have to fly in it if I didn't want to. I didn't get it – it seemed so much easier to just get a job.

Later, at the tender age of 10, I wanted…no, needed…and wanted… to make money. My mother was working several jobs just to make sure we had a decent place to live, and I wanted to help. I got an allowance but I also wanted to buy my own stuff. Yes, stuff, because what things does a 10 year old have? Records by The Jackson 5, The Osmonds and The Sylvers took more than my weekly allotment. I also genuinely wanted to contribute to the household. I knew I had a strong voice for a little girl and, amazingly, children would either be afraid of me or love me. The reality is I was not much taller than they were. I was also extremely trustworthy and smart. My mother could leave me in the house by myself (now called latchkey kid) and knew that I wouldn't get into trouble. I would clean the house, and I would have friends over without messing up the place. As long as I had my key on a chain around my neck, everything was groovy. One day my mother's friend asked me to watch her baby while she ran to the store. She told me she was not supposed to leave one minor to watch another but she had to get a friend a birthday gift. She kept *telling* me that she knew I could do it. Finally, I looked at the little thing in the stroller and said "Sure." That answer changed my life. When Ms. Toleta came back (a few hours later), she gave me $10 – an entire two weeks' allowance. Why? Because Felicia was fast asleep on the bed, bathed, fed and hair braided. That was a lot of albums in 1972. So began my first business. All because *I didn't overthink it and said "Yes." When you're young, you don't know any better. You just dive in and sink or swim.* After that episode, I found it easy to babysit more than one little tyke at a time. I didn't think about it. I just did it. When the load got too much, I just got some of my friends to help. I didn't think about it. I just did it. And when problems came up, I would deal with it.

When Peggy and I got the news that we were being let go (downsized, rightsized, laid off), we decided we would not let others determine our fate any longer. We decided to use our copiously acquired knowledge to put together a business plan, do competitive assessment, etc. Everything and everyone said the economy was bad so we should wait. But we took the dive because we knew the opportunities were available then, and if we could succeed in a down economy, imagine what we could do in an "up" economy. Now that we know what we know, if we had done more analyses, it might have scared us off from starting Consultants 2 Go. Too much research and too much info would have terrified us.

We recreated the adventure and curiosity of youth gone by. Everyone has heard the phrase "analysis paralysis" and we know what it means. *At some point, you have to stop thinking about something, and just do it – right or wrong.* You will always find reasons that sound compelling as to why you shouldn't start your business. The kids are too young, the parents are getting old, the husband wants you home when he gets home, you need a two-income household, the economy isn't right, you like the people at your j-o-b too much, you like your salary too much…*Just dive in.*

Peggy: I like to analyze things and evaluate scenarios before I make a big decision. In fact, when it comes to starting a business, I am a big believer in doing a business plan, research, etc. But in the end it still takes a giant leap of faith, and you need to just go for it. Your gut and your instincts will be just as important as any rigorous planning that you do. No matter the challenge, pay attention to your gut.

NUGGET #5 Which Structure Fits?

By Peggy

When Sandi and I left American Express, we were fortunate to have outplacement services as part of our package. This allowed us to take advantage of several classes on entrepreneurship. Several of the programs we attended included detailed discussions on the different types of business structures and the advantages and disadvantages of each. Basically, *there are four types of structures* available to the would-be entrepreneur: Sole Proprietorship, Partnership, Corporation (S and C Corp) and Limited Liability Company (LLC).

Besides deciding to start a business, *this is the second most important decision with long-lasting implications.* It is definitely a decision that should be carefully considered. While we did not rush into this decision, we could have done a better job of understanding all of the tax implications of our choice. If we had it to do all over again, we would *find a one- or two-day course on this topic*, so we were better prepared when we started the business. In addition, we would have definitely consulted accountants and lawyers more on this topic. Now, keep in mind, every time Sandi and I go for legal or financial advice, we get widely divergent views on these topics, so it pays to check with several professionals.

After consultation with our accountant, we felt that the LLC was the best fit for us. We liked the fact that the LLC was fairly low-cost and easy to establish in New Jersey, and it afforded some of the protections of a corporation. In addition, we could have the income from the LLC flow to our individual tax returns that simplifies the entire process (which is still not simple!).

An important note that we really didn't understand the impact of at the time was that partnerships and proprietorships have unlimited liability. This means we would have been personally and legally responsible for all debts and lawsuits against the business. If we had chosen those structures, our personal assets would have been at risk. I have spoken to many business owners who underestimated this risk and had all of their savings wiped out and lost their homes because of litigation and business debts. Sole Proprietorships are the easiest way to get started, so people often choose that route without fully understanding its inherent risks.

To establish our business in New Jersey, we registered our company online at the State of New Jersey's website. It was fairly easy to navigate, and the costs to form our company were less than $200. We received our approval and forms within the week. We then secured our Employer Identification Number (EIN) from the IRS, which was the next step in the process. This number is similar to a social security number, except it is for businesses. We needed this number to establish our business checking account and to file our tax returns. Establishing a separate business checking account was another crucial step in the process. We knew not to mix our business expenses and revenues with our personal accounts.

These steps were daunting at first but we discovered companies like Legal Zoom that did it for a fee. The price is different in each state, but in New Jersey it ran between $100 and $200 for their services. Because we were trying to save every dollar, we did it ourselves.

Sandi and I spent a lot of time on the business plan and operating agreement (which you need for an LLC) but I think a tax session would have saved us some heartache. *We discovered a lot of free seminars given by the SBA, SCORE and other organizations that we could have taken – so it does not have to be expensive.*

Sandi: When we wanted to do business in more than one state, it became even more complicated. We also registered in New York as we do quite a bit of business there. We will have to check the guidelines for each state in which we want to do business to see the requirements, especially if we decide to do business directly with the state or federal governments.

NUGGET #6 Choose Your Partners Wisely

By Peggy

We realized quickly that choosing a business partner is a lot like choosing a spouse. But what makes someone a good spouse does not necessarily make them a good business partner. *The type of person who is a good match on the domestic front may not be a good combination on the business side.*

I don't think I truly appreciated this fact until we started the company. As I began to think about starting a business, I knew that I would never do it with family members or friends. I had witnessed firsthand too many painful break-ups where family members or friends never spoke again because of the inevitable disagreements that occur when money and emotions are mixed.

So how did Sandi and I decide to become partners? When we worked together at American Express, we worked under pretty intense and extreme circumstances so we knew each other well. From the moment I met Sandi, I noticed that she was very buttoned up and gave off an aura of emotional intelligence and stability. This always impressed me, as did her unwavering commitment to her work and her colleagues. I could always depend on Sandi to deliver and do the right thing.

As we got to know each other at work, we realized we shared the same dream – the desire to start a business. Little did we realize that events outside of our control would propel us forward with this plan. We decided to take the severance package money and pursue our dream. We moved pretty quickly and did not spend a lot of time deciding who would be our partner. In hindsight, we probably should have considered this in more detail because the implications of this decision are so far reaching. Fortunately, this decision proved to be a very good one, and our partnership has made the business much stronger.

Sandi and I have very different skills which only enrich our relationship. We challenge each other's thinking, and we inspire each other to work smarter and better. This can be daunting for our staff, since we have such different opinions, and we can provide conflicting directions. On the other hand, we have very similar values and ethics, so our criteria for decision making, and our principles on which they rest, are always aligned, even when we come to radically different answers. The cornerstone of our partnership is built on trust, respect and honesty.

However, *because choosing each other was so successful, we were a bit cavalier and naïve about choosing an additional partner.* After a year in business, we had the opportunity to forge an alliance with another small company, owned by Mike and Rajat. They brought skills we did not have and we thought they were a good complement to our business. As a result of this alliance, we were able to win a large contract and gain a new client. Things looked great!

Due to this early success, we decided to see if they wanted to combine businesses. We asked Rajat and Mike about joining forces. Rajat said yes and seemed to indicate that Mike would too. Mike was always extremely quiet so we thought he had agreed. However, we soon realized that Mike was not on board and was actually heading to graduate school. In fact, he did not know that Rajat was joining our company as a junior partner. This should have been a warning bell but we overlooked it since we thought they were so important to growing our business.

While we assumed that Rajat would bring his current contacts, existing relationships and leads with him, he did not. In fact, he was incredibly secretive about them. He only wanted to work with us on our leads and he did not share anything with us. This should have been alarm bell #2 for us. But again, we ignored the facts. Since we didn't have this in writing in our agreement, we assumed that perhaps we misunderstood.

Another interesting phenomenon occurred during this seven-month period. All of our contracts and leads dried up. We couldn't understand it and we assumed it was just bad luck. We still had one major contract, and this client was our largest source of revenue. Dean was our largest client and had been with us from almost the beginning, even before Rajat and Mike came into the picture. He gave us a tremendous amount of work, and we kept expanding with his business. He even began discussing an alliance with our company.

While we negotiated in good faith, Rajat met with Dean privately behind our backs. He negotiated a side deal with Dean for far less money and eliminated our services. Ultimately, Rajat went to work for Dean's company, and we lost our biggest client. We felt betrayed, but we learned a lesson that we will never forget: *When our guts say something is wrong, we do not ignore it, we listen to it.* While Rajat had skills that we thought we needed for the business, his ethics were completely incompatible with ours, and he actually damaged our core business. We will never know why we didn't get any other business during that time, but we definitely know that he was a negative force. From that point forward, I only referred to him as the "albatross."

There were so many positive lessons from this experience that it is very hard for me to summarize. Now, I can use the term "positive" because it was such a valuable lesson in our journey. We were fortunate that it happened early on with our business as well as early in our relationship with Rajat. He had completely different ethics from us and we found it out within a year. It would have been far more traumatic if it took five years to uncover this trait. We also learned never to offer shares in our business so quickly. *We realized that it is much harder to get rid of a partner than an associate* and we have to really know this person well before we enter a "marriage."

Sandi: Sometimes ignorance is bliss. We knew the people with bad partnerships but if we had given ourselves enough time to really investigate why those partnerships went bad, Peggy and I would have never joined forces. Again, every book we read was against it and we kept saying it can't be all bad. We didn't start listening to the horror stories until we were well under way with Rajat.

There is an advantage to having someone with whom to bounce around ideas. Solo entrepreneurs need to find a network of other people to get this give and take. We are also never lonely in this business. The down side is that when it's time to break up the relationship, it can be brutal. I hope I have learned from all the people I've encountered who ended their partnerships. Peggy and I have updated our partnership agreement and will probably do so again even though we think it is fairly comprehensive at this point and should allow for a smooth breakup, if necessary.

A little joke about our partnership. We were at dinner with some friends of Peggy's. She had not seen them in quite some time and I was introduced as her partner. Later in the evening, someone leaned over and said to Peggy that another friend asked how long I was Peggy's partner and what happened to her husband, Robert. We forgot to use the word "business" to describe our relationship and it was mistaken for one of a more intimate nature. LOL!

My advice to a small business owner who is deciding on structure is to know the good and bad of being in a partnership before you take the leap. Proceed with caution. And if you proceed, be very upfront with your business partner about both personal and business activities because, inevitably, they will impact the overall relationship.

NUGGET #7 Open Minds...
Open Doors

By Peggy

Never prejudge a situation even when it is tempting. Our first client came from a most unexpected place. I would never have guessed that Bob would have been the first one to hire us. How did this initial success happen? Why did it seem so valuable to us and our prospects even though it was a very small sale?

Bob was a friend of mine who served on a board with me. I was the secretary of a PTA at the school my children attended. Bob was a lawyer and happened to be the treasurer on that board. Over the years, we developed a working friendship as we volunteered our time. He even reviewed my outplacement package when I left American Express with one of the other attorneys at his firm who specialized in employment law. I told him of our plans to start a business, and he provided me with some advice.

As time went on and Sandi and I began to build the business plan, I would see Bob and he would ask about the business. We told him that we were going to be a consulting firm that specialized in marketing for Fortune 1000 companies. He eventually met Sandi and asked more about how he could use our services to build his law practice. We provided him with some ideas, and one thing led to another.

Interestingly, as we had these casual conversations with Bob, we began to aggressively mobilize our lead list to launch our initial marketing and sales campaign to announce the start of the business. While we were providing advice to Bob, we began to encounter strong headwinds. No one it seemed in the corporate world wanted to be our first client. Even people who knew us for years and knew our strong track record as employees were reticent to do business with a fledgling company.

As we continued to market to corporations, Bob asked us to develop a marketing plan for him to penetrate a new industry for his business. He wanted a plan that would get his name out to key people in this particular area of the insurance industry. We jumped at the opportunity since we now realized how important that first client would be. While the fee was relatively modest, the reference was not and it proved invaluable in discussions with other potential clients. Furthermore, Bob was pleased with our efforts; he was able to secure several speaking engagements for us at the state and local Bar Association meetings. This brought us more credibility with all of our corporate leads. In fact, Sandi and I would laugh after a meeting with a prospect, because we always brought the story of Bob with us to the early meetings. When he was elected President of the Bar Association, we congratulated him and felt that we shared in his success.

Sandi and I never previously provided marketing services to lawyers. Yet, because we had an open mind and a positive attitude, we were able to get our first client and reference just as we were launching the business. While it was not a traditional path or what we had expected, it was invaluable to us in the beginning and gave us credibility with our core client prospects. Because we had never marketed to lawyers, it would have been easy to say "we don't work in that field," or "that's not our core industry." Had we closed our mind to the possibility, I'm not sure how we would have fared in those early days.

Sandi: Thank God for the Bobs of this world. If not for them, small business owners would never get a start.

As Peggy said, there are people for whom I gave my heart and soul when I worked for them or with them. I made sure that I was responsible and accountable for everything that happened when we were a team because these were people who knew my work. None of that counted when I was no longer on that team or in that company – no longer in the fold. They did not want to take chances on me once I became a start-up even though they knew my credentials. Their bosses cannot question them when they use a large consulting company of record and the project runs over budget or goes wrong. They did not want to jeopardize their jobs over our startup.

We learned not to hold high expectations from past business colleagues even if they are our friends. They are our friends only if we have expertise that they need and we can, unequivocally, increase their end-of-year ratings so they will get a bonus. When we meet new people, we treat them like they will give us business because there is a likelihood, no matter how small, that they might.

NUGGET #8 Don't Put Your Eggs in One Basket

By Peggy

As we previously stated, when we started out, we naïvely believed that some of our strongest advocates from our corporate days would embrace our new venture with open arms. We knew it would be hard, but we never envisioned how difficult it was going to be until we started making those first sales calls. People we thought we knew for years never returned our calls. People who we had helped in their jobs pretended they didn't remember us. In fact, one man I worked with for two years walked right past me and acted as if I was invisible. This was a wonderful learning experience for me and a real eye-opener. I had the gift of seeing people in a whole new light and it was both sad and exhilarating at the same time.

There were two women; one I had a good relationship with whom I thought would be helpful. She was more than just a colleague. Jessica was someone with whom I had enjoyed a solid professional affiliation. She was gracious enough to meet with us and spent some time with Sandi and me. She ran a large division for a major company and controlled all of the marketing and product development initiatives. After we spoke for a while, Jessica said she might talk to a few people, but what she really wanted to do was have us speak with a friend of hers about the consulting profession. Her friend, Tracy, was considering consulting, and she thought we could help her start her business.

While we were very gracious to Jessica, and I did meet with Tracy, she never offered to help us or make any calls on our behalf to colleagues that might need our services. When we followed up several times to see who we should contact, she was evasive, and it became clear that she did not want to jeopardize her standing in the company by becoming involved with a new business. I still believe we will get Jessica's business one day, and I can appreciate that we were too new for her to risk her professional standing with a brand new company. Periodically, we reach out to her and, as our success grows, I believe that door will open one day.

On the other hand, we met with someone who had a more casual relationship with me. She also worked in a Fortune 100 company and was in a mid-level position. Natasha went out of her way to find an opportunity for us and her boss, Woody. He was also willing to stick his neck out for C2G. We developed a proposal for them and, three months later, we moved forward with the project. It was our third deal since we started the business, and it was our largest contract to date. While it was not quite six figures, it did put us on the map, and they were our first blue chip company. It gave us a whole new level of credibility, and I would never have expected it.

Sandi: We learn as we go. We are forever trying to balance our portfolio of clients so that no one client represents more than 50% of our portfolio in terms of revenue. It is difficult to do, especially if you have an affiliation with a client. We have specific expertise in financial services and telecom and that's where we tend to do the majority of our business…and it totals much more than 50%. In the current down economy, the industry that was hit the hardest was financial services, and it could have spelled disaster for our business. We are now working to develop a clientele in other industries that are less prone to ups and downs in order to have a recession-proof company.

NUGGET #9 There are No Friends in Business

By Peggy

Every entrepreneur should repeat this rule daily! In fact, they should have their staff repeat this rule daily. Our funniest and most painful lessons occurred when we violated this rule. When you own a recruiting and consulting business, friends and family members will approach you about work. That's terrific – a referral is the most important marketing for a small business. However, you cannot show preferential treatment or bypass your procedures to help them. You still need to get any agreements in writing, and you need to make sure that your staff treats them no differently as well.

I guess this is human nature, but no matter how much I stressed this point with the team, they still continued to act differently if they knew Sandi or I had a relationship with someone with whom we were trying to do business. This led to some awkward situations. I always let my friends know that they would follow our standard procedures, including interviews with the team and complying with all our paperwork. On several occasions, friends would complain to me that they weren't interviewed or sent a contract after I promised that someone would follow up with them. The team would invariably give the same response; they thought we wouldn't make them sign our contract because they were our friends. Sandi and I both said, "There are no friends in business. There are no exceptions to our process. Everyone must sign."

When it comes to business, friends don't mix. Unfortunately, when you combine emotion with someone's livelihood, there is great potential for hard feelings that can ruin lifelong friendships. You really have to tell your friends that they will be treated the same as everyone else and that they must also follow your rules and process. If you treat them differently, it will create problems and send mixed signals to your staff. Perhaps this nugget should really be, "Treat everyone alike – strangers as well as friends!"

Sandi: Case in point. I have a good friend who really wanted to give us some business with one of our existing clients. This should have been handled in a business-as-usual process but something went wrong somewhere, and once that happened, it was hard to get back on track because that friend was now a client. My friend jumped through hurdles and hoops to get us on the project. There was an existing contract with another company who could not deliver as well as we could. She put her job on the line to get us in the door. In the end, we had to become a subcontractor for an existing vendor. To top it off, my friend was difficult to manage as a client, so much so that the consultant assigned to the project and my staff passed her over to me to deal with. In the end, the expenditure of time that I put in on the project, trying to maintain our friendship, trying to help her maintain her job, and trying to deliver a great project, was substantial. In the end it wasn't worth it. We didn't make any money on the project.

Working together with your friend as colleagues is very different than working together in a client relationship. Back then, we had a common enemy – the boss. Now, there is a role reversal, and it can be startling and unpleasant.

NUGGET #10 Be Nice to People

By Sandi

As we go through our everyday lives, we often don't pay attention to the "little people" – the Fed Ex person, the security guard, the mailman – people who are there to make life easier for you but easily get lost in the cracks. We pay more attention to the people who you want to impress such as your boss and their boss' boss (managing upwards). Something that stuck with me is to watch if the men you want to date are nice to the waiters/waitresses when you are in a restaurant because it's very telling as to how they will treat you. I find that to be true of all people. Why don't you just treat people nicely instead of going out of your way to be rude?

In business, you will definitely be surprised as to the people who will help you. And if you were not friendly or nice to them, they will remember. You never know where these people will end up, in what positions of influence they'll be in that could give you that special project. On whose advisory board could they be? Do you know who they sleep with at night when they get home? (Don't laugh because in a lot of corporations, the women don't use their married names.)

Some of our best clients came from people we were nice to years ago. We didn't necessarily know them well but we did something that they remembered. Irene, one of our strongest supporters, worked with me more than 15 years ago. We have similar personalities – direct, meaning we spoke our minds (out loud!). We connected right away. Whenever we were on teams, we always worked together to deliver a quality product. Even when we were no longer on the same team, I always checked in with her to see how she was doing. When she got promoted, I sent congratulatory flowers; I always kept in touch with her even after I left the company. There was not a lot of contact over 15 years but we knew that when one of us called, we would go out of our way to help the other. I remember when I got laid off, she was one of the first people who called me to ask if there was anything she could do for me. She also offered to be a reference if I needed one and that she would keep her eyes open for opportunities that would be beneficial to me.

When I started my consulting business, I gave her a card and asked if she ever needed help on her team to let me know. One day after I was visiting the building where we used to work, I ran into Irene on the elevator. As soon as she saw me, she said she had just asked someone for my information because it was misplaced but she needed help. That was the beginning of a large contract. She has been not just a supporter but an advocate for us. She has stood up in meetings with 40 people to say she is using us and recommend that everyone use us too. She has hired several consultants from us and is top of mind when anyone else needs help. What more can you ask for? We cultivated that relationship over years and I would never think of being mean to her.

Similarly, years ago Peggy gave a ride home to a colleague. They were at a business party and it was late. The colleague would have taken the train home and not gotten home until after midnight. Peggy offered her a ride since she was going in the same general direction. She thought it was just a nice thing to do as it was so late. During the ride, she got to know this colleague a little better and found out that they had a few things in common. Peggy sporadically called on her when we started our business, and they exchanged business cards.

Over six years later when that colleague left the company to work for a much smaller start-up, she took Peggy's business card with her as one of the key people she would need to reach out to if she needed help. Of course, we were one of the first people she called when she had a project that was not being delivered on time and needed help.

I don't think that our company would have been top of mind if it wasn't for that fateful day that Peggy made the decision to be nice to a colleague.

It takes the same amount of effort to be nice as it does to be nasty. The old adage about catching flies with honey is true. I've learned that when someone is being deliberately mean to me, I can still smile (clients are always right...right?). Being nice is different than having someone walk over you. If they are being mean, give them the feedback in an even, firm tone so that they know where you are coming from, and then you never have to deal with them again if you don't want to. Remember, things are said about you and your company when you are not in the room and you should behave in the same manner in which you would like things said about you.

Peggy: What goes around comes around. If you are nice and treat all people with respect, it will come back to you in many positive ways. Even if you have a business disagreement with someone, you should still maintain a professional demeanor and not get personal. In the end, you are creating your own personal brand, and how you interact with colleagues, service personnel, bosses, bankers and neighbors will all form part of your brand reputation – be sure it is one that would make you proud. If someone was describing you when you were not there, would it make you happy or flinch?

NUGGET #11 **Beware the Naysayers**

By Peggy

Like attracts like. At least that's the view of many popular books today. This looks to be a difficult year so the last thing you need as a business owner is someone focused on the negative. That doesn't mean you are ignoring significant trends in your business, industry or the overall economy, but it does mean you focus on how you can be successful and capitalize on those trends in bad times. It means reinventing your business or services so that it can meet the challenges ahead but it does not mean dwelling on all the bad that is out there.

We once had a newly hired salesperson who started off with a real bang. He got appointments with prospects that we had no luck with for more than two years. We were impressed with his cold calling techniques and overall ability. In the first two months, we thought we had a real winner. He had several close calls and was negotiating two deals in August after only two and a half months. Unfortunately, both deals fell apart in the worst way – they went the slow death route. The client was all action in the beginning and then suddenly stopped returning phone calls. This pattern was repeated several more times, and it was frustrating for all of us.

After six months, we began to realize that perhaps Tom wasn't as good at selling as we initially thought. We realized that he was still struggling with understanding our business and perhaps the clients sensed that he really didn't understand their needs. However, his cold calling continued to wow us. Unfortunately, Tom told us that he really didn't like doing cold calling. We also started to notice that he became negative and somewhat defensive. His job was a "hunter" and he needed to break into new accounts for us.

He started to resent our "farmer" or account manager who worked on our existing business. He asked to become an account manager instead, but we told Tom that we needed him to get into the accounts first before there was something to manage. We didn't need an additional account manager. As time went on, he still continued to get great appointments, which is really hard to do in our business. But he couldn't close a deal. He started to blame us for his failure and became increasingly more difficult and negative. We kept hoping he would learn our business and things would improve. Unfortunately, his negativity spread to others on the team, and ultimately we had to end the relationship. We should have moved much more quickly, and we will the next time we have someone who threatens to bring the whole team down.

This is also true for friends and family members. If you have people surrounding you who are not supportive of your business, keep them away from it. That negative energy can really impact your psyche and hurt your efforts. If they are friends, you can still socialize with them, but don't discuss the business. If they are close family members, this can be more difficult, but you need to figure it out before it harms you. Owning and running your business is very difficult, and success defies the odds. You need to have all the enthusiasm and positivity in order to maximize your chances so that you can beat the odds!

If we only had one Nugget, this would be it. Get rid of the "Debbie Downers" in your life – those who see the glass half empty. Owning your business is hard; don't make it harder on yourself. You need every ounce of your positive energy going into your business – don't let anyone destroy that or it will kill your dream faster than anything!

Sandi: There are poisonous people whom you should absolutely get rid of. You will have to learn how to weed your garden. I don't think we can ever truly get rid of the naysayers. We just have to manage them. You can't get rid of your family – who may be some of the naysayers – but, by your actions, you can change their minds and win them over to your way of thinking. And if you cannot, just leave them out of your business and let action speak louder than words by becoming a success.

NUGGET #12 **Fear and Failure**

By Sandi

Fear is a big part of being a business owner. You live with it daily, and the root of all business fears stem from finances. You're afraid that you won't make payroll this week; what if you don't get any sales in the funnel? Can you afford the rent or will you have to give up your space and work from home?

Your biggest failures will be because of the things you are afraid to do. But you must still operate your businesses and you cannot let fear get the best of you. The thing that will make you move forward or make you fail is the ability to take fear into consideration and put it aside in order to execute.

We wanted to increase our team. We really needed salespeople as it was difficult to sell while we were delivering projects ourselves. We kept putting this off for months until it was clear that we would either grow or go out of business. There are only 24 hours in a day and two hands to do the work. We started by securing a line of credit so we had something on which to fall back. As soon as we got our salesperson, we started to see the value in having an additional person. We could have made that move a long time ago but we were afraid to take the chance.

When we wanted to move from our home office, it was the same fear that kept us home for just a little bit longer. And we probably would have stayed there being too afraid to take on rent. Luckily for us, we explored all our options and found that we could limit our liabilities by subleasing space from our trademark lawyer.

At the time of this writing, we're afraid of this recession and what it has done and will do to the business. It is a very real fear but that doesn't mean we are giving in to that fear. We are going to work harder than ever and make more sales calls than ever.

Everyone has fear – we would not be human if we didn't. However, I find that African-Americans have a lot of personal fears – we're afraid of the cold, swimming, heights, flying. Perhaps it's because we have been told for a long time what we can't do, not what we can. My own personal routine for confronting things for which I'm afraid is to a) write down the pros and cons and b) make a judgment call based on my list to see if it is something that makes sense to tackle, then c) go tackle it piece by piece. Anything can be done in 15 minute increments. You can do it too.

Peggy: As I said in the first chapter, I was afraid of failing and taking risks. Now I realize that failing can be one of the most enriching life experiences. I have learned the most from my biggest failures – like losing a job. Often the fear of the failure is worse than the experience itself. Once you get over the emotion, it is always good to reflect on what worked and didn't. This reflection is a key contributor to understanding how you would handle things differently in the future.

NUGGET #13 **Put It in Writing!**

By Peggy

One of the key lessons we learned in the first two years was to put everything in writing. This is particularly important when you are negotiating client contracts, partnership alliances and consultant agreements. I know as a hurried entrepreneur it seems to take more time upfront, but it will save a tremendous amount of time and trouble at the end. If you spell out your terms and conditions clearly in writing, it will really help you understand what the other party is thinking and give you some genuine insight into their character and skills.

Here are two things that happened to us in the first two years that really illustrated how important it is to practice this discipline. Remember Mike and Rajat? As part of our relationship, we did negotiate a Memorandum of Understanding with them on the terms of our alliance. This was before we invited Rajat to be a junior partner. What we never clearly defined was how many customers each party would bring to the relationship and if current or existing clients would be part of the alliance. We introduced them to our current clients and prospects, and we assumed that they would do the same thing. After several months, when they kept meeting with our customers but we never met theirs, we realized something was wrong. Rajat was pretty clear – he said they never intended on bringing their existing relationships to the table and we were wrong to assume that this was part of the agreement. We didn't spell it out in the document since we assumed it was mutually understood and we learned a very valuable lesson from it. They never brought any customers to the deal and by then, we had lost our negotiating leverage since we had successfully signed a new deal with one of our clients that required their skills. Lesson learned here: Don't assume, and get it in writing!

As a result, once we did bring Rajat in as a junior partner, Sandi and I both felt that we needed to create a formal agreement that was very detailed and contained specific termination language. Raj would have preferred a more informal approach, but we realized that it was not in our best interest. This proved invaluable in the following year when we realized that he negotiated a side deal with our largest client. We were able to act very quickly and sever the agreement. The terms were incredibly clear on revenue sharing and ownership, and we always maintained majority control so that we could terminate the agreement on minimal notice.

It would have been far more difficult to remove him from the business if we had not had a specific and detailed agreement in place. If you are considering these types of agreements, do your homework, get counsel if necessary and consider the terms you would like in place if the alliance fails. I know we all hope these deals will be successful but you should envision how you want to control things if they go sour. This will help you define the most important terms in the agreement and your escape clauses that will allow you to exit when necessary. One final note – don't allow people to begin working with you until the deal is done. People will always be more willing to agree to your terms before you provide them with some benefits than after. No one should talk to a client or begin any work until the ink is on the document.

You can't be too careful when it comes to negotiating. Be sure to be clear, and don't dance around the difficult or contentious issues. They will only come back to haunt you later in the relationship. We learned a lot from these situations, and now we have all of our arrangements – alliances, client contracts and consultant contracts – in writing.

Sandi: Sometimes it seems a done deal when you are working with people you know. Or you say, "We'll discuss that later. Let's just get the deal done before we are out of time." But when money is involved, you realize you never really know someone. And you never find this out when things are going well; it's usually during a dispute.

Lena, a member of my women's group said, "A contract is like a condom – I never leave home without it." This is very true as you should have a written contract for everything you do, regardless of how small the opportunity.

NUGGET #14 Networking 101: Ten Nuggets for Entrepreneurs and Job Hunters

By Sandi

When I started my company seven years ago, I was told I better start networking. This term conjured up all sorts of images in my head. I pictured people running in a maze, racing from person to person gathering business cards. I now realize that true networking could not be further from this image. In fact, I didn't realize it then but I had been successfully networking for many years. I just called it something else – volunteering in my community. When I had this breakthrough, I began assembling a list of tips to share with other novice networkers so they could learn from my experiences.

1. Start Networking as Soon as Possible

Start networking well before you start your business or before you need to find a job. This does not mean that you only join business-related activities. Peggy and I were both involved in philanthropic and school activities that we were interested in and had nothing to do with our business. However, we formed strong relationships through these organizations that proved beneficial when we started the business.

2. Follow Your Interests

Don't get involved or join groups just to get something from them. Join the group because you are truly interested in what they do and more importantly, you want to help them be successful. This is how trust and collaboration are developed.

3. Build Deep Relationships

It is far better to join one or two organizations where you really become active and get involved than join 20 organizations where you only attend a meeting or event once a year. Getting involved is the best way to build long-term relationships with people, and it's through these relationships that opportunities will emerge over time.

4. Collecting Business Cards Does Not Make You a Good Networker

We have all been at events and meetings where someone comes up to you and thrusts a card at you. They've barely heard your name or introduced themselves when they start waving a card. Please don't fall into this trap. Collecting 20 cards from people you can barely remember is not effective or productive. Stop and connect with each person you meet at the event. Ask genuine questions about them and their background. Spend 20 minutes or more with someone you really enjoy and in the end a true connection will be established. Remember it is quality not quantity that makes you successful.

5. Don't Call Someone You've Just Met and Ask Them for a Favor

Successful networking is all about helping others. It's about relating and working with others with whom you share a mutual interest or connection. Don't squander the connection. Nothing is a bigger turn-off than the person who calls you after you've just met and wants to pitch something to you right away. Typically, the receiver of the pitch wants to hang up or run away and usually stops returning messages. Rather, enjoy the relationship and let it develop over time.

6. Practice Your Elevator Pitch

Practice your elevator pitch before you go to your first event or meeting. At these networking events, use your pitch. If people don't understand what you do in one minute or less – go back and rewrite it until they do. These meetings and events are a great place to get immediate feedback on how you are doing. People will usually let you know if they don't "get it."

7. Even the Shy Can Be Successful

You will probably need to practice your elevator pitch a little more. Choose a friend or colleague whom you feel comfortable with so that you can practice your technique. Before you go to your first event, set a realistic goal for how many people you will meet. Tell yourself that you will meet one person at the event and you will make a genuine connection with them. Your goal will be to connect and arrange a future meeting. After the event, assess whether you were successful. If yes, raise the stakes for the next one, and see if you can do better. Go back to your friends and practice a little more. With practice comes confidence and success.

8. What Can I Learn From These Experiences?

Joining organizations and volunteering on a committee are great ways to learn a new skill. If you have never done sales, try the solicitation committee for the fundraiser or raffle. If you want to learn marketing and public relations, helping to promote an event or fundraiser can give you practical experience. I definitely honed my sales skills when I was soliciting local merchants for donations and gifts in my town for my local school's silent auction. If you're a recent college graduate, don't hesitate to work on your college's annual fund. This can be a safe way to learn the sales business.

9. Host a Party or Dinner in Your Home or Office

This can be some work but it's very rewarding. It's a very powerful and intimate way to create stronger connection and bonds with people since you are opening your home to them. I have done this on many occasions, and it has proven to be one of my most powerful networking tools.

10. Have Fun

Finally, relax and have fun. It is far more rewarding if you do things that you like. People will sense it and everyone will relax around you.

How to Work the Room

Remember the old adage: People buy from people they know. Build your networks by developing mutually beneficial relationships with people!

Utilizing all of these tips, I can walk into any room and start or join a conversation – the problem is, sometimes I just don't want to engage. I remember taking a Dale Carnegie class many years ago on how to speak to anyone and learning that people have certain topics in common to which we can relate and speak with ease.

The key commonalities that can get you through most evenings without clearing a room are:

a) where we live

b) where we were born

c) where we went to school

d) our families

e) music

f) food

g) trips you have taken

h) our jobs

i) hobbies

Topics that will ignite the room in flames are:

a) politics   b) race   c) sex

I keep the above topics in my head and can easily navigate from one to the next depending how the conversation is going. Think of other topics that can get you through a night without uncomfortable silences. One topic will lead you to another.

Peggy: I know this is a cliché but another topic that breaks the ice is sports. I am not a sports fan but my husband and son are fanatics. Through osmosis, I am fairly knowledgeable about the latest news in sports. I find this is also a great way to break in to conversation, particularly with men (although not exclusively). Networking is the lifeblood of any small business, and everyone can do it with practice. It just takes getting out there!

NUGGET #15 Maintain Your Contacts

By Sandi

When I was in corporate, I hardly did any "networking"...I had a job and career. Why would I need to network? When I was asked to attend a conference, I made so much noise about falling behind in my work that they were forced to send someone else. Forget trade shows! What horrors – to sit in a booth all day and have people who have no interest in you come by and ask you questions about things they had no interest in buying.

I remember one particular trade show in Las Vegas. One of the more senior executives could not attend and called on me at the last minute. I did not want to go, but I was the only available person. On the flight, I connected with two other participants from my company who were attending the same conference. Even though I didn't want to go on the trip, I decided to make small talk with these two women who became my life savers, filling in for me at the booth and giving me critical information that I didn't have regarding our product.

I've tried to stay in touch with those ladies even though we are not all in the same company anymore because that was a time that bonded us. Whenever I see them, we are always friendly to each other.

Little did I know that it was my responsibility to maintain contact with people when they left the company. Some were truly my friends, but I'm really talking about the acquaintances whose homes you never got invited to, or the ones you never invited to your house, but you saw each other for more hours in the day than you saw your children or your spouse. They are the ones who, if you needed someone to work late, or someone to give you critical information, would come through for you in small ways that proved to be big.

Stay in touch with people when they leave your job, your business, your school, etc. Peggy is a master of staying in touch with people. She naturally has that certain thing that I didn't have but have since learned – the gift of gab and small talk. When she meets you, she asks about your children, pets, what school you attended, your parents' name and where they live…ya da…ya da…ya da. All the Networking 101 questions! Low and behold, she'll realize that you both attended the same school, that your parents come from her hometown, that you married someone from a rival high school. This information, inevitably, surfaces when she has to reach out to you, especially if you have left the company where she is or she can't find your phone number. She can get in touch with you through your high school alumni association, call your mother from the home town directory…whatever, but Inspector McHale will find you.

I'm much better at this in an organized setting, but her built-in Dale Carnegie training is amazing. She will really remember all this the next time she meets you or hears your name. I have to work at it. It can be scary when someone who hasn't seen you in 15 years and who you don't remember starts to spew off facts about your parents, children or pets.

In this age of technology, "small talk" is easier. Use social media (Linked In, MySpace, Plaxo, Google Friends, etc.) to stay up to date with people whom you have not seen or have lost touch with. Profiles allow you to know where they are working and uploaded pictures let you see what their families look like. I'm learning how to tweet, connect and anything else that is out there. It takes practice but it does help.

Peggy: I have a pretty good memory for facts about people. I don't consciously do it but, somehow at key moments, I can remember vivid facts about the person whom I am meeting or about to call. This has served me well because most people are very flattered if you remember this type of information, and it almost always helps you to connect with them. I happen to have a good memory but you don't have to in order to recall these facts. Just jot down and store them in your contact database or, if you are still paper-based, your day timer. That way, the next time you reach out to this person (which could be a year or more later), you can add a personal touch to the conversation.

NUGGET #16 Marketing – Creating Your Roadmap

By Peggy

When we started C2G in 2002, we were focused on developing both the business plan and marketing plan. These are two essential ingredients for success. You need a roadmap to chart where you are headed; otherwise, you will never know where you're going and how to get there. However, most people think of them as some large book with hundreds of pages that get shoved on a bookcase somewhere. This couldn't be further from the truth. They should be concise and manageable so you can update them regularly. The marketing plan does not have to be more than a few pages, and it should include a budget and calendar of your marketing activities. Sandi and I routinely update both documents so that we always have a handle on what our marketing goals are, what we will spend and a calendar of our activities.

But I can't tell you how many entrepreneurs I meet who do not have a marketing or business plan. And, surprisingly, they will not do it or hire someone to do it for them. Yet, they will spend money on desks and equipment without thinking about it. These two tools are far more important to success than any tangible asset like a chair and a desk because this really defines your business, goals, target customers, pricing and how you will sell your product or service.

When we began our company, we realized that the most important marketing tool was our company website. While a brochure is good to have, we really spent our time creating our site. We were fortunate because Sandi's cousin, Dennis, was in the business, and he guided us through the process.

He developed our initial site, and we wrote all the copy for it. It took about a month for us to get the first one up and going, and we did it with minimal cost. Another lesson here – it doesn't have to be perfect. The beauty of a website is that you can change it very quickly. Unlike a brochure that can cost thousands to reprint and update, a site change can be done with minimal time and expense.

As part of our marketing plan, we determined that we needed to build our brand and credibility by getting some local press. We also wanted to have some articles published to establish our credentials in our field. We interviewed several PR professionals and selected a woman in New Jersey who used to run the Governor's communication office. She had many contacts in the state, and we thought she would be a good fit for our needs. As we were solidifying the contract, we were notified by the Women's Business Center that we were the recipient of the Entrepreneur of the Year Award. One of our earliest supporters, Penni Nafus, had nominated us and we were selected as the winner. This was exactly the type of newsworthy event that can get you noticed in the press. Because we had a plan, we were able to act immediately when good fortune struck. We were prepared to capitalize on this significant achievement.

We went to the Awards luncheon, and we invested in the day. We purchased a table and invited several of our largest clients to the ceremony. Our publicist was present and had her camera ready. We were interviewed by the business reporter for the largest newspaper in New Jersey, The Star Ledger. We were featured in that paper as well as several weeklies and even appeared on Cable News. Interestingly, we were picked up on the American Express website and featured to all 75,000 employees because the article mentioned our former employer – another good way to get free press without spending more money. Yes, we spent about $2,000 on that day, but the press that we received was worth thousands more, and we established our name with several reporters who continue to call us now when they need quotes from small business owners.

Sandi and I also became shameless awards junkies after this event. We saw the power of them and the coverage you can garner for your business. This led us to an even bigger opportunity two years later, but that took a plan and preparation before it materialized.

Success doesn't happen due to luck. You have to plan and figure out how you are going to succeed and then, when something good happens, you are able to maximize its value to the fullest extent. While winning that award was lucky, and it wouldn't have happened without our champion Penni, it proved to be a turning point with our start-up. It got us noticed and vaulted us to a new level.

Sandi: Because we saw the lack of marketing and business plans in small businesses, we created a class called Marketing Plan In A Day. It gives all the critical factors that a small business owner needs in a marketing plan. The owner takes the class and brings their financials, a computer and current marketing material. At the end of the class, they have some tangible information that they can actually go back to their desks and use.

We also have a one-page business plan that we use. We purchased a book of the same name (*One Page Business Plan*) and use this as a quick reference for ourselves and our team. Marketing and business plans are tools of your business. They are meant to be updated on a regular basis and not just be used as bookends on your shelves. A good time to review to see if you are still on track or if something needs to be adjusted is at your quarterly review and strategic planning sessions.

NUGGET #17 Winning Awards – The Secret to Free PR

By Peggy

Marketing success doesn't happen overnight but is typically a well-planned campaign. In 2004, when we won the Entrepreneur of the Year Award from the Women's Business Center and the New Jersey Association of Women Business Owners (NJAWBO), we received tremendous publicity from state and local publications as well as local cable news. We realized that we were on to something. As a result, we decided to devote some time to researching business awards and applying for them. It was while doing this research in 2005 that we learned about "The Make Mine a Million $ Business Contest." It seemed like an award that was custom-designed for us, and we really wanted to apply. So Sandi and I plotted our strategy so that we could enter and win this contest. We researched the opportunity by reviewing the website, assessing the requirements and developing a plan so that we would be ready in 2006.

We went to the New York contest, held at American Express' headquarters in December 2005, to see how the actual event was structured. We were wowed by the enthusiasm of the participants and the people who ran the contest. Nell Merlino, the founder of Count Me In for Women's Economic Independence, is a true visionary who developed the concept of the contest. She has tremendous drive, passion and commitment that is infectious so she is able to persuade others to join her in these philanthropic endeavors. This contest was her "baby" and it provided a host of tools and prizes for women-owned businesses. The winner would receive a generous $50,000 line of credit from Open at American Express.

We sat there in the auditorium in December 2005 in awe. This contest was exactly what we needed to get our company to the next level – the million dollar revenue level. After that day, we went back to the website and registered our interest in the program. We now understood what it would take to enter and make the finals. Our financials needed to be in order. We needed a clearly defined business plan and we needed to demonstrate how we would use the array of prizes to grow our business.

That August 2006, when we both received the email saying the contest was now open for the New York event, we knew we were ready to enter. Only one of us could be a participant, so we decided that Sandi should be the contestant. She submitted all the paperwork and in early October, we were notified that she was one of the 30 finalists in the contest. There were over 1,200 applications, and now we were going to be in the big show.

Much had changed in a year. The contest grew in popularity from 2005. It was now held at the Manhattan Center with over 1,500 attendants. Featured speakers were Hillary Clinton and Suze Orman. There was a large number of reporters and press coverage for the event, including TV, business magazines and newspapers. American Express was their main sponsor and leveraged their massive marketing power to get PR for the organization.

As part of the contest, each business owner had to deliver a three-minute talk and tell the audience how winning would help their business. The audience and the judges would vote on each presentation and decide who the winners would be. The pressure was immense. Sandi prepared her pitch on the red-eye from London, returning from a funeral for her favorite uncle, Carleton. She went straight to the two-day event from the airport with no sleep. The speech coach Hillary, provided by Make Mine A Million to all the finalists, ripped her first draft to shreds – and offered to introduce her to a smile since she was a bit cranky from her ordeal. She went home that night and completely re-wrote and memorized her speech for "game day." Still no sleep! All our friends were there and caught up in the exciting atmosphere of

The Apprentice meets American Idol.

When Sandi gave her three-minute pitch, my heart was pounding and I locked hands with Valda, Sandi's mom. We were both so nervous. Later that evening, we burst out with applause and cheers when Sandi's name was called as one of the winners. I felt like we had just won the Miss America pageant.

That night, we were interviewed by a host of reporters. We received so much press from this event. In fact, Sandi was featured on the cover of Money Magazine. More important, that year, we almost tripled our revenues to hit the $1million mark. A lot of it came in the fourth quarter. The momentum received from winning and the advice and coaching that we received from the program certainly helped us to reach this milestone.

After that, we went on to win several contests and awards. It has proven a big help to our small business and cannot be matched in terms of what we would have to pay to get that press.

Sandi: This is my story and I'm sticking to it. I was operating on pure adrenaline and didn't care if I won that contest at that point. Peg tried to cheer me up and reminded me how hard we had worked and what it would mean to win – that was the one time that I was close to feeling hate for my partner. Somehow, it started to sink in but my motivation was when I saw all the press, and yes, noticed that there were very few African-American women in the contest and that was fascinating to the press. Essence Magazine was there (every black girl's dream) and the competitive drive in me made me get up, smile and bring my A game.

I was one of the last few names that they called. I could hear Peggy screaming that we won and there was a blur of people saying congratulations and taking pictures. I think I uttered, "Can I go to sleep now?"

It was definitely one of the highlights of being in business. We developed a wonderful relationship with the Count Me In team as well as with the other winners.

Bottom line – the lure of very real PR will make you become amazing!

NUGGET #18 Flexibility –
The Key to Survival

By Peggy

Flexible: *capable of being bent, usually without breaking*
Adaptable: *able to adjust oneself readily to different conditions*

Cited from *Dictionary.com*

If the only constant in this world is change, then only those who can change will survive. Therefore, as small business owners you must be adaptable and flexible if you want to succeed and flourish. That's why I like the definitions cited above, particularly "bending without breaking." That is the embodiment of being an entrepreneur. As I said in an earlier chapter, planning is crucial to the successful business owner. However, it does not mean that those plans are set in stone; remember, they are a map not a monument. You need to adapt on a moment's notice and update your plans accordingly in order for you to capitalize on opportunities or to avoid negative trends. You always have to know when you need to change and modify your approach.

In our early years, we only did fixed-priced projects. We noticed that our projects had a very long sales cycle. While they were very profitable, we found that it was difficult to close these types of deals quickly. The sign-offs for these projects were often at a very high level within the company. We needed a vice president or "C" Suite member to concur. As our cash dwindled, we knew we needed to find something else to even out the peaks and valleys. Providing interim marketing resources seemed like a way to obtain quicker decisions and thus quicker cash. So we made the decision to move forward with this service and trialed it in 2005. We were correct with our assumption that securing agreements for this type of service from clients was far quicker to obtain. We could usually get an agreement approved within weeks as opposed to months with a project. We were now typically dealing with more junior people who were empowered to make these budget decisions without requiring higher approval.

It was this change that allowed us to survive. In fact, by making this change in 2005, it was the catalyst that allowed us to grow by almost 300% in 2006. We made the right decision and we were able to close a significant amount of business as a result. If we didn't do this, I am not sure we would be around today. While we still do projects as well as provide interim resources, the quick pace of these sales really accelerated our growth and provided the cash flow that is the lifeblood of any business.

This was a pivotal learning moment for us when deciding if we could really make a go of our business. We had many debates over this topic, but we were convinced this was where we needed to make the change. We tested our concept, learned from it and reaped the rewards as a result.

Sandi: Peggy brought the idea of staff augmentation to my attention. We both noticed that it would take forever to make a sale and, as she said, we were running out of money. I was ready to send out my resume but we also realized that both of us could easily get consulting assignments when we needed it to bring in cash. Peg had previously worked in the IT arena, and this business model held true there, so we had very lengthy discussions about how best to execute on this. We were both in agreement as we saw the model worked when we were in corporate and hired individual consultants far more quickly when we needed them than to put in a Statement of Work for a project. We also looked at some of our past assignments and realized they may have been negotiated as a project, but in reality, it really hit the staff augmentation line item on our clients' budgets.

So, as in the *Taking Risks* chapter, do your homework when you need to be flexible. Do the research so that you are well-versed in your company's strengths and weaknesses and understanding of how flexible you can and need to be. We are also not advocating that you bend so much that the rubberband snaps! *You can't say "yes" to everything that comes your way in the name of adaptation and flexibility.* You must learn when to say "no" to things that are totally outside what you do as a business.

You have to be flexible and not stuck in your ways – the business and trends determine what you need to do. Don't stick to your original grandiose ideas if they won't work. This sounds counter to us saying draft up a business plan and stick to it, but we truly believe that your business plan is a living document that you change as the needs of the business change, and as the economy changes. The economy waits for no small business but flexibility can get you through it.

NUGGET #19 Take Risks – Place a Few Bets

By Sandi

Both Peggy and I are risk averse. We don't mind taking risks but they have to be extremely calculated. Sometimes it's good, and sometimes it's bad. But no matter what you do in your own business, you will have to take some big bets on projects, people, time, etc. And you hope these bets pay off.

A Bet that We Were Not Willing to Take:

Everyone told us that in order to get a line of credit, we must put up our homes. There are no two ways around it. That was not feasible to either of us, especially since I'm a single head of household, and I needed to keep a roof over my head. It's not a gamble that I could feel good about. Peggy felt the same way, and we decided that we would explore other avenues of obtaining a line of credit (LOC) or loan without going into hock.

The first path was to get a line of credit from American Express. We applied and received a $7,500 line, which was a good start but not what we wanted to get us through any upcoming rough spots. Second, we also knew that American Express was a sponsor for the Make Mine a Million $ Business program that we won. We applied for the $50,000 line of credit that was offered as one of the winner's prizes. We received it, and that gave us a measure of confidence.

Then we researched local banks that were friendlier to small businesses than the larger chains. Valley National Bank was one of them. We applied there and received a line of credit. We applied to our credit union and received another one.

We were slowly growing the amounts of money that were available to us. The money was also spread out so we didn't have any one place that was holding too much credit for us.

Good Risks:

When we decided to create new services like training, delivering courses and creating packages for small business owners, we knew we were taking a risk moving away from the core business area; however, they were calculated risks where the outcome would not devastate us. Also, we ensured that the services are complementary to our current skill set. We were not opening up a catering business when our core was marketing services. If we needed business and our new services did not work out, we could move on to other services. The courses were also topics that we heard from our consultants. We were not making a judgment call that this is something that they don't know they need.

Peggy is the one who will analyze things 50 ways to Sunday before going ahead. I admit, I will analyze, but I'm faster to react on certain things than Peg. Either way, we see failures as a way of learning what to do and what not do; what risks to take and ones that probably should have been thought through a little more.

So, there are good risks and bad risks. We beg you to minimize your exposure, while trying something that is not within your norm or your comfort zone.

Peggy: I think the recent financial crises vindicated our thinking on why we were not willing to put our houses up as collateral. We didn't think it was a necessary risk and still don't. We chose to secure credit in other ways and expand our business through organic growth. On the other hand, we knew hiring a sales person was going to increase our overhead. Yet, we were willing to take this risk since we felt it was the way for us to accelerate our business growth.

NUGGET #20 Maintain an Impeccable Reputation

By Sandi

Your name and your credit are all you have. Together, they create your reputation. When you lose those two things, you have nothing as a business person.

Losing your credit by paying your bills late is creating a bad reputation with your creditors. These are the same people that you must go back to when you need money. Why should they give it to you when you have a poor track record of paying back?

You need to ensure that you pay your bills on time even if you can only make a minimum payment. If you cannot make even the minimum, call the creditor. Most of us run the other way and avoid the creditor which only makes them more persistent and less agreeable to any terms you may want to propose.

Losing your good name is worse than losing your credit. If people think you do not have honesty and integrity, you may as well take down your shingle. A good name can help you get good credit. If your banker gets a great reference from your clients, they will be more prone to take a chance on you because of what they hear.

When we place consultants on assignments, they represent us. Our name is forever associated with them even when they come off assignment. The performance of that consultant is how the client will remember us – good or bad.

We got a call from one of our strongest advocates, letting us know that they needed a consultant immediately. We asked one of our consultants, Jackie, to take the assignment. Her resume said she had an extensive background in direct marketing. Unfortunately, she was at a higher level (VP) in another company and never did hands-on marketing. After a few months, the assignment became unbearable, and many problems arose. I had to step in to save our name. I had to work extra hard to overcome the perception that our company did less than perfect work. This made it even more difficult on me since I had to to erase a negative impression and do great work at the same time.

Our good name is all we have – and all you have…and it's as good as money in the bank. Your personal credit is intertwined with your business credit, and if you have a partner, their credit is now mixed up with yours.

PR can make or break the name of your business. Obviously, when you are generating press, you do all you can to ensure that your name is reflected in a good light. If you have no control over how or when your name will be mentioned, do everything within your power to ensure that it is in a positive light.

When you send your team out to represent you, they present a business card with your company's name on it. If the client has a poor experience, the reference will most likely be not to use the *company*, whereas if the client has a good experience, they might remember the individual.

Do everything in you power to maintain your good name.

Peggy: I think we are also judged on how we handle things when they don't go well initially. I think most people will give you a second chance if something gets screwed up. When things go bad for whatever reason, you need to act quickly to fix the situation for the client or the creditor. Life is never perfect, but it is how you deal with problems that is really important. Our client and colleagues saw how determined we were to fix the problem when our consultant was not a good fit for the project. We were determined to get the project back on track and did whatever it took to make the situation better. I think we were able to restore our reputation as a result. People knew we cared and that we wanted to deliver the highest quality. Sometimes things go wrong but it is how you recover that is often judged the most critically by your peers or clients.

NUGGET #21 Hire Slow, Fire Fast

By Peggy

Hirings and firings are always the most difficult decisions because they directly involve people. Our biggest worries and longest discussions are always on this topic, but one thing became apparent to us over time – that once you hire someone, you can usually tell within the first 30 days if they are going to work out. One of the first salespeople we hired was Sissy. She was a lovely woman with a good resume. It indicated a solid background in sales and marketing, a seemingly perfect fit for us. Up to this point, we were having a tough time finding a qualified person who wanted to be involved with our small start-up company.

Sissy interviewed well and provided us with her references. However, a little alarm bell went off in my head when she was unable to provide a name of a prior boss – someone whom she had directly reported to in her previous experiences. She explained that they all had changed companies and she lost contact with them over the years. I found that a bit odd, that in sixteen years of working that not one boss was still around somewhere that we could speak to about her skills.

However, despite my anxiety, her other references checked out so we offered her the position. She started setting up sales calls with different individuals and we realized that she didn't quite understand what we did. We reviewed all of our materials and discussed our core capabilities with her, but she always seemed to be unsure of what we did and why.

Finally she asked to have a formal training session in our office. We thought this was a great idea, and we invited the whole team to be present. She kept pushing to have the class, and she worked on setting it up. The day of the class, it rained lightly. As we sat in the office, Sissy never came. After about an hour and a half, she called from her cell phone and said that she hit traffic and decided to turn around and not come. She did not apologize or offer to come late. She said it was too much effort. This was alarm bell two! Both Sandi and I thought something was wrong but we still allowed her to work for us.

After about two months, Sissy set up a meeting with a warm prospect that I referred to her. Jim was someone that Sandi and I both knew from our corporate careers. We had enjoyed a solid professional relationship with him and we thought he was a good lead for Sissy. She coordinated the meeting with Jim's assistant, and we decided that the three of us would meet in front of Jim's office. That day, Sissy decided to go ahead and enter the building without us. She was already in the conference room meeting with Jim when we entered the room. I smiled at both of them, and she ran over and gave me a big kiss hello and hug as we sat down. This was definitely alarm bell three going off! I had never been at a sales call where the sales person greeted their boss with a kiss hello. Anyway, she kicked off the meeting and began to describe all of our services incorrectly. She still didn't get it, and fortunately we were able to jump in and save the meeting. After that fiasco, Sandi and I decided we would terminate our arrangement with Sissy. We really should have told her that we needed a reference from a direct supervisor before we hired her, and today I direct all my recruiters to ask for references from at least one supervisor.

We still talk about Sissy and her impact on our hiring practices. She was a lovely woman, and we didn't want to hurt her feelings. But when you are in a business, you need to deal with problems quickly. It was clear she was not going to work out within the first 30 days, and we should have acted decisively then and not waited. It was not going to get any better even with training! *We should have taken more time up front to hire her and then fire her faster.*

Sandi: I've not read the book about being nice in the corner office but I can surmise that we were stricken with that malady. Niceness and not wanting to hurt people's feelings are two of the flaws of small business owners, and women in particular, regardless of color. We want to be fair. We want to leave the relationship on a good note, not burning any bridges. I say that we need to be fair to ourselves and to our employees, our consultants and to our clients. Having an unproductive person drags down everyone. We all have to do more damage control and more work just to stay on par.

Once we let go of our salesperson, we saw that there were good things about her, but overall we didn't really miss her. How can you have a salesperson and not miss them? You should ask yourself that question about your team. Who would you miss if they left, and why? Whose presence corresponds to revenue for you? Who are the people who are just nice and, therefore, nice-to-haves? It will be amazing once you have it on paper.

We use this analogy constantly in our decision making. "You are on a boat in a river in a storm. It's about to capsize and you have to push people overboard. Who is the last person you would keep to go down with you on the boat?" The answer helps you to decide the most necessary people on your team besides you. If you can't find an answer, then you will need to slowly rebuild your team!

NUGGET #22 Hire Thinkers and Doers

By Peggy

We made two significant decisions on hiring in a one-year period. Annette came to us in early 2005. She was hired to work on a small project that involved both sales and marketing for one of our largest clients. She did a terrific job and actually demonstrated her ability to do sales even though she had no prior experience. We asked her if she would consider doing sales for us on a continual basis. Originally, she said no because she did not consider herself a salesperson. In time, we were able to demonstrate that a good salesperson knew her product or service and can effectively communicate that to a potential client. Once she accepted, she proved to be a key member of our organization and is with us today.

Her ability to think out of the box and provide dual roles as a sales leader and a marketing specialist proved invaluable as we grew our company. When we need something done, whatever the task, she is willing to step in. Annette is the epitome of the thinker and doer and we were fortunate that she joined our team.

Conversely, I hired a former colleague to help on the very same project a year earlier. She was a really nice gal that had been out of work for quite some time. To help her out, I offered her the opportunity to work on a project that we had. She seemed initially grateful and excited to be working, but as soon as we started rolling, her enthusiasm waned, and she did not follow through on many of her tasks. Even after much prodding and guidance she became evasive and unavailable. I think she might have been depressed, and while I wanted her to be a success, it simply was not going to be the case.

As women business owners, we want to "mother" or nurture some of our team members. In fact, one business strategist referred to them as the "wounded birds." I think that was an apt description for what I was attempting to do. But this is a classic mistake that many business owners make; we think we can help people out with a job even when it is clearly not in the best interest of the company. I wanted my bird to succeed, knowing in my heart that it was probably never going to fly. In the end, we simply did not use her on future projects. The learning here is that in order for you to be successful, you have to make decisions that are right for the business. Using your company for charity is noble but can lead to some big problems. What you really want is a company that is so successful that you can make generous donations to those causes that you believe in.

Trial and error is part of the process when you own your own business. This was another step in our evolution – you need to hire the best and the brightest and not look at your business as a way to solve friends' problems. In the end, it won't work, and it can cost you the friendship and your business as well.

Sandi: I classify people into three buckets – whether correctly or incorrectly:

1. There are definitely people who are strategists (*thinkers*); they think at the 10,000-foot level and usually start their sentences with "I have a great idea!" They can play out different scenarios of what they think will work, and many of them are good, sound ideas. But when you try to execute some of those ideas, you fail because all the consequences were not fully thought out.

2. Then there are others who are not comfortable thinking of an idea to save their lives but once you ask them to execute an already established idea, they are fantastic and will run with it. I call them

worker bees (*doers*.) They will stay until midnight on Christmas Eve to ensure a project comes to fruition. You call them on weekends, early mornings and late nights at the office and they will pick up the phone. Yes, they need the money but they get immense satisfaction at bringing in a project on time, on budget and from simply doing a good job.

3. Last, there are people like me (at least this is how I classify myself). I was a worker bee who became a strategist. I worked my way up through the ranks learning how to execute brilliantly. In the process, I would identify strengths of that plan and opportunities for improvements ("corporatese" for all the stuff that's wrong with the plan). These types of people easily straddle the line between the two worlds. I dare to say that Peggy is also in this bucket, as well as Annette – in different degrees, of course. We're *straddlers*! We know what it takes to do the job and because of that, we can devise strategies that are actionable and able to be executed.

Organizations need all three types to properly function, but I must say, in a small business where you have limited resources, those straddlers will come through for you every time. If you look at the types of people who are the most successful with our company, they are the ones who can write the proposal, sell the project and then execute it, if necessary. That's what you want also.

NUGGET #23 Train Your Team

By Peggy

The most important thing for you to do is train your team on your values and inspire them to work as a trusted team. This sounds easy, but this is one of the most difficult and important things you must do as a leader. When we started the company, Sandi and I wanted to apply the sound lessons we learned at AT&T and American Express. We both had significant experience managing large groups of people, and we had received considerable training over the years. We wanted to incorporate these teachings into our own business but give them our own personal twist.

Once we started adding consultants, we decided to institute quarterly business reviews. At first, we would only share our top-line revenue with the team, but we realized that it was important to share our profitability as well.

Second, we wanted our team to understand our core values and work ethic. We needed them to understand how we did business so they could perform in a manner that was consistent with our philosophy. For us, being trustworthy, dependable and not taking short cuts on the quality of the work are very important attributes that all of our consultants must share.

Several years ago, Donald joined our firm as a consultant. He had great credentials and references; however, his work style was inconsistent with our core beliefs. Donald took an assignment with us that turned out to be a poor match. Compounding the problem, he would often take short cuts with his work. We quickly realized that Don should not continue. Fortunately for us, Don could also see that we had a different style and approach to doing business, so we were able to part ways in a fairly agreeable fashion. We finished the assignment with our client so that we could deliver at the level that we wanted, and Don was free to work elsewhere.

This was an important lesson for us and our team. We recognized that how someone works and their methods to accomplishing a task are also vital to our success. Our team also gained a greater appreciation for evaluating potential consultants on these criteria. It underscored for them the importance we place on our ethics and philosophy and what is required when someone acts on C2G's behalf. Since all of us at C2G "lived" this lesson, it was a powerful shared experience. The beauty of this lesson was that our client was extremely happy with our efforts and our commitment to deliver in spite of the circumstances. The mid-stream change in consultants did not damage our relationship. In fact, because we jumped in to manage the situation, they saw it as a great benefit.

The client did not demand the change; we recognized the situation as a result of some quality checks we made on Donald's output. He was working in a way that was inconsistent with our standards. Fortunately, he also realized that it was not working out and wanted to leave too. While we needed to react quickly, I think we all realized that someone who does not share our values about our work would never be a good fit for our company. In fact, the longer they stay, the more it can damage your culture.

Sandi: You can do but so much vetting, especially when you start to work with individuals who are outside your network. You never worked with them, and their references are stellar. So it is up to you to ensure they receive training. As a consulting company, we cannot really give training to our consultants in terms of what they need to do the job, but we are obligated to giving them direction on how they must represent our company. Lately, we have gone the extra mile in delivering presentations such as "Basic Principles of Consulting," based on feedback that we have gathered over time on the traits of superior consultants. Additionally, we have guided them to courses that would give them the necessary skills that they need. For example, our consultants must have a particular level of skill on PowerPoint and Excel and that is expected by our clients. If we have a consultant who is lacking in a particular area, we are good at delivering that feedback so that it helps them as individual consultants but also accurately reflects the C2G image of what a client can expect in our consultants.

As a small business owner, you may not have the financial resources to send your employees to training. It is necessary. Many small business development centers and women's business centers offer courses free of charge. Send your team to them. The government (state and federal) also give training classes on business development if you're selling to the government – it can be used anywhere. If you are located in an Economic Development Center, similar to the one in which we are located at NJIT, and it is sponsored by the state, you will receive an abundance of training as a part of your lease agreement.

If all else fails, be creative and barter with other experts for training. For example, a restaurant that needs an employment manual can cater an event for a HR specialist in return for customizing a manual. Be creative.

NUGGET #24 Open the Kimono – Share Your Finances

By Peggy

I think one of the biggest mistakes most business owners make with their people is being secretive about the finances. We fell into this trap too. I think it is human nature to be guarded about your money and not reveal too much information. Here's what we learned and why it's important to tell your team what's happening in the business.

Sandi and I were like most business owners – keeping the wraps on our finances. We only told our team what they absolutely had to know. Once we hit the $1 million mark in revenue in year three, our key people began to assume that we were taking all the profits for ourselves. We could hear it in their comments about our "earnings." Every time we said we were reinvesting it in the business to pay our added people, you could tell that they were not buying it. They felt we were not letting them share in our success. It became adversarial at times with the team, particularly when we were discussing our commission plan and other compensation-related matters.

Fortunately, we belong to several women's support groups that focus on female presidents and entrepreneurs. The advice we got was to share your numbers with your team so that they understand your margins and how you make money. We realized that we needed to do that, and we started hosting formal quarterly meetings where we reviewed our current performance and talked about our goals for the upcoming quarter and year. This made a tremendous difference with the team. They saw exactly how the money came in and how it went out. They stopped questioning us and began to feel extremely invested in the business. Their suggestions and improvements about the business were usually insightful and on target. They really wanted us to succeed so they could succeed.

Complementing this approach was the addition of Doug, the CFO to the team. He added credibility to the discussions and provided valuable tools to help us better assess our strengths and weaknesses. This elevated the discussions we had and kept the team focused on how we improve revenue, increase margins and minimize expenses so we can all share in our success.

There were many insights gained from this experience. People want to be part of a team and feel trusted. When you share information that they understand is confidential and important, they will respond in a positive way. We built a better team because they realized how much we invested in them for the business, and it made them feel valued.

Sandi: Yes, I do work like a maniac, and sometimes I like it. But really, this is my sole income, and I work hard so that I don't have to get a side hustle (extra job, for those not in the know). Because it is our business, I try to deliver to the best of my ability. When our team didn't understand the numbers – that if Peggy and I didn't work, we would not have enough money to pay their income! – I did receive a lot of comments about how hard I worked. I think it was more in the vein, as Peggy said, that we were making all this money and not sharing. We were becoming frustrated and touchy.

We always discussed sharing some information, but I also think it gave us a sense of control to have the numbers when they didn't, childish as that may sound (the "we're the boss" syndrome). We would share some with one person and a different piece of info with another, but no one besides us had the full picture. The team was friendly and talked among themselves so they were piecing things together, and it didn't always add up.

The Make Mine a Million program was one of the first programs that advocated sharing your numbers…and once it was talked about in our own business owners' group, it didn't seem so scary after all. We decided to take the leap. Gosh! Why didn't we do this before? I actually saw the light bulbs go off in their heads, and the numbers were thoroughly scrutinized and questioned, but we had answers for them.

The change that this brought about was phenomenal and really helped us to grow our business. There were times now that they questioned if we were the best people for the project even though they knew it was a necessity for us to work. Everyone knew their main job was to keep Peggy and me working. It was not a matter of choice assignments at top price but of any assignment to keep the business going. The team was so invested that they just wanted the best people for the job.

I also have to add that even though we were sharing numbers, when we brought in the CFO, it brought an immense amount of credibility with our team to have an "outsider" being surgically focused and unbiased about the numbers. There were no questions as to what needed to be managed (euphemism for "cut") Everyone knows the margin we need to get, the sales we need to achieve and, correspondingly, the consequences of not doing so.

In a downward economy, this shared knowledge has helped to sustain us. We were having the best year yet. It was the best of times and the worst of times. When the phones stopped ringing, our team understood taking a decrease in hours. I will never say they were happy about it, and I can never say we were happy about doing it. But I do believe that full disclosure of our finances made it easier for them to understand the decisions that had to be made.

Our learning was that you can't call yourself a "team" if you don't share the vital pieces of the business. And nothing is more vital in business than the financials. If business owners can understand that, it would take a lot of stress off the individual owner and place it squarely on the shoulders of the team.

NUGGET #25 Create the Company Culture You Want

By Peggy

Sandi and I are working moms. We both know what its like to be at a meeting and get the call from the school nurse. You are worried about your child and the boss who might not care about your family responsibilities. When we formed C2G, we knew we wanted it to fit our lifestyle requirements. One of the great joys of owning the business has been my ability to "blend" my day so that I can attend a client meeting in the morning then rush to my other "client," Emily, and take her to dance lessons. I can come home, make dinner and then hit the email and work for a few hours. While I certainly don't work less hours, I am able to do it on my own terms. This had made my life less stressed and I only have to worry about getting the work done, not getting face time with the boss or the team. We wanted to share this philosophy with our consultants.

As a result, we created a company that is a completely virtual organization that utilizes the resources of our talented pool of independent consultants. Our entire business model is built on creating a virtual pool of resources that can be deployed on a moment's notice. Our consultants provide us with their unique requirements, and we find projects based on their needs. They let us know if they are available for full-time, part-time, on-site or virtual engagements. They provide us with their fee structure, and we negotiate on their behalf. Even the core functions within C2G, like sales, recruiting and accounting, are performed by independent consultants from their home offices.

C2G attracts two distinct types of consultants – working moms and bridge workers (ex-pats or retirees from corporate America). Both of these groups desire *flexible work arrangements* that will give them greater personal balance in their life. Our projects are customized to their needs so that it can fit their lifestyles. As a result, we have been able to attract an incredible talent pool, and personal referrals are our number-one source for new consultants. We have over 250 consultants in our network, and our retention rate is well over 85%. All of our consultants have 10 or more years in their field, and most have advanced degrees from top universities. Since all our consultants are independent, our entire culture is driven by entrepreneurship and ownership.

C2G's company culture and business model have been extremely instrumental in facilitating our growth. The expansion of our network was possible because the demand for flexible work arrangements by these highly skilled consultants continues to grow. Since our model addresses this fundamental need, we have been successful in recruiting and retaining the talent. While we do not use a traditional employee-based model, we are definitely filling a niche in the marketplace, and the growth of our consultant base supports this point.

More important, this is who we are! I have two children, and when I started the company in 2002, Robbie was 13, and Emily was 9. I realized how unhappy I was in my great VP job at American Express because the role put me at odds with my need to manage and take care of my family. It was my desire for a flexible arrangement and a need for a "blended" approach that drove me to form the company.

My prior experience at AT&T showed me that a blended life is possible since I was allowed to work part-time for four years. This worked well with glowing reviews until I had a boss who decided he wouldn't let that arrangement work. Once he took over as my boss, he decided within two weeks that I needed to be full-time – immediately. I had no choice if I wanted to keep my job since the company always made the decision to be flexible at the discretion of the supervisor and needs of the business – that's where the seeds for C2G were sown.

Nugget #25 Create the Company Culture You Want

Sandi: I have raised my niece, Lauren, since birth so, like Peggy, I had a teenage girl in the house. If you have ever been the parent of a teenage girl, I need not say another word about that. I, too, needed a flexible work arrangement. She was in junior high and was preparing to enter one of the best high schools in New York. In order to do so, she had to take one year of prep classes at the high school. Someone had to pick her up at school, which was on one side of Brooklyn, and transport her to the high school, which was located on the other side of Brooklyn. Then pick her up to return home.

I understood Peggy's plight and was ready to take on the task of being the chauffeur for Lauren and her friends. Working from home allowed us to really have some family time, as well as work on projects where we did not have to be onsite at the client. We did have rules about being professional, but sometimes that went out the window as our families did not abide by those rules. We tried to not have background noise (cats screaming, children fighting, husbands whistling...you get the drift)! We did not mind when our consultants had background noise with us but never with a client.

In order for virtual assignments to work successfully, we had some ground rules for our consultants.

- Try to be in a place where you can speak freely. If you are not in a location where you can speak freely, let the phone go to voice mail.

- Have access to a computer when speaking to clients, if possible, because you can review documentation when the client speaks about it.

- We also used our cell phones as our main contact line since that made us always available without the client knowing where you are. If for some reason you have to use your home phone, make sure the number is blocked as you don't want the entire world to start returning calls to your home where a child can pick up the phone.

- When creating your corporate culture, put rules in place. Everyone on your team should be on the same page about what is expected from them and what to expect from you.

In our organization, we try to foster a culture of openness, professionalism, honesty and flexibility. We hope we have been successful.

NUGGET #26 Relationship Management – Handling Difficult People

By Sandi

It is practically a law that you will not like everyone with whom you come in contact. That includes family, friends, associates, clients, employees, and consultants. The only person who everyone liked was my grandmother, and I'm sure she didn't like everyone either.

Women are always told to be nice, and there is nothing wrong with that. We discussed that in another chapter. There is a difference between being nice and being stupid. Being stupid means you say things that you will regret because it's your largest account, or walking away from dollars that are sure.

We were presented with a situation where we didn't like the client and we still had to perform at a superior level. This client was referred to us by a trusted coworker, Benjamin. Besides Ben, we were in a unique position where we were the only other consultants who had the skills that were needed. We immediately landed our first out-of-town contract. We were brought in to work on the strategy and analytics component that would form the backbone for future marketing campaigns. Our client, Dean, owned the agency and had no expertise in this niche and, therefore, was dependent on us. At the time, we did not know that the future of his entire account was dependent on our excellent delivery. Dean was extremely happy with our work but made sure we knew upfront that this was his client and did not want us to speak to the client without him. He was afraid that the client would find out that we were the subject matter experts and would demand that we participate on future projects.

Dean started becoming obnoxious half-way through the project. He would leave us out of critical meetings with the client. He also did not miss a beat in letting us know that he started his company at the same time that we did but was doing multi-million dollars in business, implying we didn't know what we were doing. Dean also started to nickel and dime us in terms of our contract. He would have his pit bull VP not pay some bills and disputed work that was already delivered and agreed on – he would try to change the amount and payment terms.

We still had to deliver for Dean because the end user was a much larger bank. Our reputation would have been on the line and we could not just walk away from this project. We knew several people who worked at the company or who had deep connections there, and it would not have looked good for us to just throw up our hands with Dean.

After the project was closed out, we severed our relationship with Dean. It ended when he offered to buy our company; and when we declined, he joined forces with our junior partner, Raj, and hired him away from us. Turned out to be a blessing for us.

The point is we were so upset towards the end of the project and could have just thrown up our hands and walked out on Dean. We recognized that there will be plenty of Deans in our lifetime. We left with a great reputation for delivering superior work – even Dean wanted to work with us again! We didn't have to like Dean but we did have to work with him. Deans come in many forms – they can be someone with whom you are working.

A similar incident happened with one of our consultants. She had done smaller projects for us, and we felt fairly comfortable putting her on a much larger assignment. A key concern was that she traveled from Philadelphia each day to work in New Jersey. She assured us it would not be a problem. But it did become a problem. She was driving hundreds of miles to drop her daughter off at school and then to come in to work. The relationship started to deteriorate when she told us that the assignment was becoming too troublesome and that she was thinking of leaving. We were upset since we had a client agreement to uphold with a fairly new client.

At the same time, we discovered that this consultant was writing a proposal in our company's name but to sell her own product. A nasty conversation ensued where we asked her to cease and desist, and we remained calm while the consultant literally cried and ranted and raved. That is not the way we operate our business, but we made sure the project was successfully completed.

Our main issue was, regardless of our feelings toward the client or consultant, we resolved these matters in a way that it doesn't damage either the client or C2G. We did not let client and consultant disagreements get in the way of doing a good job. As for Dean, we knew we would not do any more work for/with him. When he calls, we are busy. As for the consultant, we no longer use this person and made a decision that we would never place this person on another assignment.

Peggy: Decide what you want the outcome to be before you deal with the people you don't like. We knew we needed to work with Dean since we were a relatively new business. We also knew that in spite of our feelings for him, we needed to perform flawlessly, which we did. Two years after we worked with him, someone from his team contacted us about working on another project since we still enjoyed a sterling reputation. If we had delivered poorly or if we gave in to our emotions and quit midway through the assignment, we would have destroyed our reputations, and our hard work would have been for naught.

NUGGET #27 Sales, Sales and More Sales

By Peggy

No matter how many great sales people you hire, as a business owner you need to be able to sell. I don't care what line of work you are in; this is a key ingredient for any successful business. And if you have no experience, you will get it the day you open for business. So start looking for sales training to get better at it. Remember, there are many low-cost seminars and events that can help you with sales. Get referrals from other small business owners and successful salespeople you meet. I find people are always willing to share a resource if they found it helpful.

One of the first tools in your sales arsenal is your elevator pitch. Many times, if you don't get this right, you lose potential prospects and leads right from the beginning. That's because, as the business owner, you are selling your business at all sorts of places such as networking events, seminars, board meetings, etc. You need to clearly and crisply say what your business does. I have to say that we struggled with our pitch for more than two years. It was when we clearly defined our core business that we finally got it right. It still evolves and will continue to as we change our services, but our fast pitch has been the same since 2005.

I am known as a pretty big talker, but I have learned to shut up and listen. I have learned the power of silence. On sales calls, I now ask a lot of questions and let the customer do the talking. I try to guide the discussion, and I always look for an opportunity to close business, but I am a copious note taker. As I take notes, I practice "active" listening, to try to understand what the client really wants and needs.

After any call with a client, I always follow up with an email or a handwritten note. I don't become the annoying salesperson that calls every two days, but I do create a touch strategy so that I have regular contact points at different intervals using different channels (email, notes, phone and events) so that I continue to communicate with the prospect.

We called and met with one potential client, George, for many years. We continued to market to George and sent him reminders. Last year while I was on vacation, George had someone on his staff reach out to us. He knew what we provided, and he was calling to see if we could discuss a potential project with him. We prepared a proposal for George and the deal closed in 30 days. It was a six-figure contract. It took us three years to land this blue chip account, but persistence paid off!

No matter how many times people tell you to give up, you should never do it. We worked this account for many years with little success. We followed our plan and reached out to the prospect at regular intervals, every other month or so. Then one day, out of the blue, he called, and we landed a large contract. All those years of reminding him about our business paid off.

Sandi: Sales is another tough area that very few people like to do. The people who can do it well are a rare commodity. Every business person has to be their own best salesperson. You should be able to speak about your business on a minute's notice. If you don't know what you do, how can you teach your team? Make no mistake that others may become more fluent at it than you are, but you should have all the answers.

There are many good sales training courses available, and you can take what you need from each of them. I always learn something new. Having a script when you call is helpful. I keep bullet points in my head of the top three things that I need to say when I'm speaking to a potential client.

Without sales, you have no business. We do get a lot of our business from referrals; however, that runs out fairly quickly. It's amazing how quickly you can go through the warm leads that you have. Sooner or later, you will have to pick up that phone or make some kind of contact with people who don't have a clue what you do – I call it descending into cold call hell! But it must be done. As I write this, I know I have to finish this chapter in about one hour so that I can make my five calls for the day (25 per week is our goal).

It can get discouraging, but know there is a light at the end of the tunnel. All you need are a few "yeses," as one of them will turn into a bona fide contract.

NUGGET #28 Sales, Sales and No Sales

By Peggy

This is probably one of the funniest encounters we had in business, and it happened early on. A good friend of mine recommended a salesperson to us who she wanted to help. The person had recently lost his job from a large company and needed work. Earlier in his career, he had been a good salesperson, so we were ready to give it a try. Vito came to our office and interviewed with both Sandi and me. He told us he was very excited about the opportunity and that our firm's culture and virtual organization would fit well with his lifestyle. He mentioned all the contacts he had and how he could leverage them for our benefit. He also mentioned something else to us that we should have seen as a big clue, but we ignored it (yes, yet again) since we knew he needed work. This was 2005 so we were still learning that "wounded birds" won't help the company grow.

Anyway, while Vito never mentioned his commission requirements or financial needs, he did share with us that he had been to a psychic, and she had told him that he was about to enter a significant relationship with an African American. Vito felt this was a good omen for him to work for us. While we chuckled about it, we still brought him on to do sales.

Weeks went by and Vito kept requesting time to travel. In the two months that he worked for us, he spent four weeks in Paris and three weeks in San Diego. We did go to one business lunch where we met with mutual colleagues about business. I picked up the tab, and that was the extent of his sales work with C2G. He called us the next week and said he realized he needed more time off so it was probably not going to work out. I guess that lunch really tied him down.

Moral of this story: Don't hire people who tell you that the psychic said it was a good idea that they work for you. More important, don't hire salespeople who don't talk about money, appear uninterested in earning it and don't seem really hungry. We have since learned that the people who make the best salespeople are those who are really motivated by money.

I try to remember all of these lessons from this story:

1. Don't ever bring on a person in any capacity as a favor. They should be qualified and have the skill sets you need.

2. Women have this natural interest to nurture and bring on wounded birds. Your business is not a charity; treat it like a business.

3. Most important, when hiring salespeople, make sure they bring up money in the first 10 minutes – otherwise, they are not cut out for sales!

Sandi: We don't always take our own advice, and it always comes back to bite us. This will happen several times before the bell rings in your head. We learned that there can be such a thing as too much flexibility; this was to the point that nothing got done.

I recall Vito talking to me more about his golf games and where he has played throughout the world than what I recall him saying about sales. This was someone who was at a high level in corporate and came to us highly recommended. He was just not at a point in his life where sales was what he wanted to do first and foremost. Sales would have been a by-product of his golf game. And frankly, I was not at a point in my life where I was interested in having him live his psychic dream through me.

I also learned that a lot of busy work can be done that results in no real sales effort. Of course, I can't shortchange any salesperson by not mentioning that there are a lot of times that busy work will be done and the result is not of their making – projects get placed on hold after you have spent too many hours working the account, your contact gets downsized, etc. This is why we like to have a contact funnel list on our shared drive that can be viewed by all so that we know if our team is actually making calls, and if not, what we can do to help.

NUGGET #29 You Won't Get Business If You Don't Ask for It!

By Sandi

This nugget could also be called "The Tale of Two Genders" since women and men behave very differently when it comes to asking for business and helping each other out.

When we started out, we were making presentations to everyone and wondering why we were not getting the business, especially when everyone said they "loved our presentations." Finally, we got advice from several strong sales professionals, and they told us you must always *ask for the business*. What a revelation! When we finally took the advice and learned to ask for the business, we were able to quickly close several sales.

We were also reluctant to leverage the "old girls network" and, quite frankly, I believe the network for women is still young and maturing and needs to be nurtured. Women want to help but I think we are still learning how to help each other collectively so that we can all be successful. (Maybe this reluctance comes from years of competition when moving up even one rung on the ladder took so much effort.)

However, once we started to tap into our network and began to ask for the business, we were able to close our first big opportunity. It was a direct result from a woman who Peggy knew from a previous job. Gayle worked for an IT company that wanted to find out more about pharmaceutical companies with whom they wanted to do business. It was a growing, mid-size company that did not believe in marketing. The head of sales, Roger, who called a lot of the shots, clearly stated in front of us that he didn't believe it ever works.

Nugget #29 You Won't Get Business If You Don't Ask for It!

He thought it was a complete waste of time and money. Gayle, who headed up operations wanted to bring us in despite the blatant misgivings of Roger. She knew they desperately needed to break into that market and needed a winning market strategy to be successful. We were at the top of the list to do the job for Gayle, but first we needed to convince Roger and ask for the business.

We interviewed several key people at the firm and looked at the industry. We prepared a thorough analysis of the situation on what should be done. We pitched it to Roger, and we were able to convince him to give us a try. We definitely asked for the business and he gave us the green light. Gayle also supported us by affirming that we would go above and beyond to get the job done for them.

The moral of the story: You will not get it if you don't ask. By the way, Roger left that company and started his own several years later. He and Gayle called us back in to help on the marketing strategy for the new venture. He also had no problem asking his network for the business. He was able to secure a multi-million dollar contract within the first month of being in business. How was he so lucky? He called up his buddy, who worked in a senior position at a major Fortune 500 company and was placed on the vendor list. He called his other buddy at the firm and was able to bid and win on a major project. The "old boy network" alive and well!

Peggy: We have a lot to learn from men on this topic. Don't be afraid to ask for help from your network or be shy about wanting to make the sale. We now always ask clients and prospects if they want to move forward on every sales call. We are no longer timid or shy on this, and we have really leveraged our network to open doors for us. However, you must also be willing to reciprocate and help your "buddies" as well!

NUGGET #30 Once You Get Business, How Do You Price It?

By Sandi

Women are notorious for not asking for the business and then not asking for enough money. Here's our quick lesson in Negotiation 101.

a) **If your client doesn't negotiate with you, your price is too low.** When we wrote one of our first proposals for our client, Dean, Peggy and I debated what our final price should be. We came up with a price that was satisfactory to both of us and put that in the proposal. We really wanted to win this business since we were only in business a short while, so we knew we were very conservative in our pricing. We kept negotiating down our price among the two of us and really underpriced our services by about 50%. We should have had a clue when Dean did not even bat an eyelash at the price and hired us right away. Later, we learned that Dean marked us up significantly and also landed a multimillion dollar contract from the work we did at a very low cost. The fact that he thought we were a steal was exactly that.

b) **Be willing to know what you will give up. How low will you go and what is high within reason?** Before negotiation begins, you should have an idea of where you want to come in at the end of the deal. What will you give up with your clients vs. what will you have to give to them. We were not prepared to deal with Dean as we didn't have the answers to the above questions. We knew that we wanted this contract. At the time, that was the most amount of money we were going to be paid for a project. We thought we would come in on the lower end as that would bring us more business with Dean. That was a big mistake as the low price was the price that Dean always remembered in future negotiations. We could never raise our rates with him as a result. This was a key learning moment for us: Once you set a price point with your client, you are often stuck with it for the duration of your relationship! So beware.

c) When you are putting together a proposal, ensure that you know the price your competitor is asking for a similar service or product. So we didn't know what price we should come in with for Dean. We had very limited information on what we should charge for this type of project. We thought our final price was fair. We later discovered that he was able to mark us up by over 100% with the client. Dean was not going to tell us that as it was an opportunity for him to get great service and knowledge at a low price. His profit margin was huge.

We have learned that you always give yourself a little legroom when negotiating. Know your price, then go a little higher – not unreasonably so but enough that if forced to come down, you will still be in a good place; add 10-15% on top of where you want to come in. When we asked for a line of credit at Valley National Bank, we asked for more than we thought we needed. That is just in case we didn't get what we asked for, we would still come in where we needed to be. If you get what you asked for, it measurably increases your profit margin. If you come in at the right price, you will still cover your margins.

Peggy: I think this is probably the area where we have shown the most improvement since we started the business. In the beginning, we would second guess ourselves. Now, we are definitely more decisive in our approach, and we understand the margin we need to make. We always benchmark our services against our competitors too.

We also got a lot smarter when negotiating for human resources. In the early days, we would be negotiating with the client and the consultant. We quickly realized that this was a recipe for disaster, so now we already have our terms agreed upon with our consultant before we ever start pricing a deal for a client. You can never have enough practice and training in this area, so keep working it!

NUGGET #31 **Angels**

By Peggy

Angels are people who drop out of the sky to help us with no strings attached. Free resources, friendly people and helping hands abound for the would-be entrepreneur. All you need to do is keep an open mind and do a little homework. We were incredibly focused on finding free classes or low cost networking events whenever and wherever possible. We routinely scoured the internet and checked local business publications like *Crain's New York* to see upcoming classes and events.

A perfect example of our thrifty ways was when we needed to learn QuickBooks as soon as possible. We were counseled by our accountant that this was the #1 choice for managing the company's financials so we purchased a copy at a discount through our local warehouse club, BJ's. I called the Women's Business Center in New Jersey, and they offered a class for free. They also provided free counseling services for our business to help answer some of our basic start-up questions. Penni Nafus, the Director of the Center, met with us at the local library. We showed up with our laptops! We walked through the start-up process for QuickBooks and basically created the company's profile right there. It was a tremendous help, and she was able to answer some of the stickier set-up questions for QB. Along the way, she became one of our many "angels" who provided us with help and assistance when we needed it. As we stated, an angel is a person who will give you help without asking for anything in return. They're one of those people who do things out of the goodness of their hearts…and they continue to help you anytime you call them or need them.

In 2003, we had the opportunity to bid on a proposal for Penni at the

Women's Business Center. You will be amazed how one so-called "lucky" or fortunate event led to another. After several rounds of submissions on our proposal, we were chosen by the committee as the winner of the bid. Our job was to create a marketing strategy and plan for the center. We couldn't believe it – we had won a blind RFP. We jumped into this project with gusto and created a plan that was on target for what they needed. At our final meeting, we were expected to present to the WBC Board and their parent organization, New Jersey Association of Women Business Owners (NJAWBO). About a month later, impressed with our work, NJAWBO asked me if I would be interested in joining the State Board as their VP of Marketing. After some thought, I decided to run and was elected to their 2004 Board.

Working on the Board was a great opportunity, and I have built relationships with other women business owners that I still have to this day. And if you recall, it was Penni who gave us our first big media opportunity by nominating us for the Entrepreneur of the Year Award. Isn't it interesting that all of these subsequent opportunities came from just taking advantage of one free resource as we were starting our business?

This is probably one of the most unexpected delights of being a small business owner – you never know what good things are waiting for you. That's why it is so important not to pre-judge situations. Take advantage of all the free and low-cost events and classes you can, you would be surprised at how helpful they can be, and you never know who you will meet there.

Sandi: The first time I heard the term "angel" was in connection with the angel investors – a team of people who will invest in your business, mostly for a piece of your business. We have presented to angel investors even though they were not looking for marketing businesses, but we thought it would be a good thing to get practice and learn how to put together an investor presentation. Unless your small business is a product business or an IT-type business that can bring in incredible returns on investment, you are not likely to get an angel investor.

What we have found is that you can find angels in many forms. You do not have to give up a piece of your business. Look for people who will develop an emotional investment in your business. They want you to do well and believe in you. Your doing well reflects positively on them. So, for Penni, her good deed in helping us also reflected well on the Women's Business Center – we can be held up as a model member who received help from them.

Your angels can be on your board as well. They can give you guidance that is incomparable to financial help, and they don't want anything in return. Angels can be in the form of a satisfied client who becomes an advocate for you and passes your name on to other potential clients who can utilize your products or services.

Cherish these angels and show them appreciation. These good deeds are priceless.

NUGGET #32 **Incubators**

By Peggy

Opportunity knocks in the strangest places. Does this sound like a constant theme? You bet! Sandi and I both knew we needed to trademark our business name and logo, so we consulted with Bob – our first client. He suggested that we talk to Mike (his wife was also on the local school PTA with me.) Yes, it is a small world. Mike's specialty was patent and trademarks, so we thought he was a good start for us. He reviewed what we wanted to do and said that the whole process would take about a year if there were no challenges to our mark. His fee was nominal so we decided to proceed. We met with him in his Newark office since it was closer to my home. His one office was based in a business incubator on the campus of New Jersey Institute of Technology (NJIT.) As part of his agreement, he provided assistance to some of the firms located at the incubator. An incubator is a place that houses small business owners who are in the fledgling stages of their business with the hope of helping them to grow that business.

Mike also had an office in New York City and was thinking of giving up his New Jersey space. While we were working with him on our trademark search, we also noticed that we were beginning to outgrow our normal meeting place, Starbucks. Up to this point, we held our meetings and interviews at one of their many ubiquitous locations. However, we realized that it might now be time to get some kind of space. At one of our discussions with Mike, he asked us if we would like to sublet an office from him. We looked at the cost and decided that it was affordable and said yes. Although we were subletting from Mike, we still needed approval from the incubator.

They sent us a lease, and we signed on for the space in Newark. This was

2004, and a lot of people questioned why we wanted to be in Newark. We saw this as an opportunity to get space at low cost in a nice facility. Yes, Newark had its issues but it appeared that the state and the city were serious about turning it around.

Once we were there, we soon realized what a great opportunity this was. The incubator, sponsored by New Jersey Institute of Technology (NJIT), with support from the New Jersey Commission of Science and Technology, offered a great deal to its primary tenants. They provided mentoring, resources, access to student interns and seed grants.

This was a terrific place to have our business. We also knew that as soon as we could do it, we wanted to become primary tenants. In late 2004, Mike said that he was planning on leaving. He wanted to know if we wanted his space. We looked at the cost and realized it was too much for our budget. We approached Lou, the Building Manager, to see if there were any low-cost spaces available.

After a review, he said he had one 450-square-foot space that used to be the lunch room. He would get it ready for us, and we could have it for about $495 a month. In an incubator, many times the rents are kept at below market rates for a period of time as businesses are just starting out. As they mature and prosper, the price per square foot increases for the space. We realized that this was a bargain, and we jumped at the opportunity. While Lou apologized about the sink, which was a holdover from the lunch room, we were delighted with it. Now, we could make hot chocolate (Sandi's favorite) and coffee (mine) whenever we wanted. Being thrifty, we offered a flat price for Mike's office furniture and we were in business. We never looked back.

Once there, we took advantage of all the resources offered by the Enterprise Development Center incubator. We received several seed grants that paid for our new brochure, an updated website and recruiting. A significant benefit of the incubator is the mentoring and coaching that we receive on an ongoing basis. We have tapped into free legal resources, business consultants and the broader NJIT college community. We have participated in Capstone programs where the students, under the direction of a tenured professor or faculty member, helped to design our recruiter database and made enhancements to our business processes. Another group of MBA candidates provided a comprehensive assessment of our business plan. Finally, the peer-to-peer mentoring and collaboration with the other eighty companies in the incubator was a tremendous benefit as well.

My advice to any new business owner is to research if there is an incubator in a nearby area. Keep an open mind about locales. We went to Newark, and it has been a tremendous benefit, but I know a lot of people who would not have considered it because of the bad press the city received. We have a great location with security and features for which many other places would charge much more.

Sandi: Like going to Newark was a big deal for a Brooklynite! Please! When we started looking at the idea of incubators, I did my due diligence on possible incubators in New York. The only one at the time was in the Bronx. Bronx…Newark…Bronx…Newark. What a tough choice. Well, the rent at the Bronx location was double what was being asked in Newark. Newark is also halfway between Peggy's home and my house, so it was a no brainer. Also, the Bronx incubator did not offer some of the same amenities and accessibility as did Newark, and there was no mention of seed grants. I also found that there were some colleges in New York that offered space to small business owners – the company that hosted our website at the time was in one such location; however, they are not called incubators as they do not offer a lot of the other amenities.

Peg and I tossed around the idea of renting an old fire station that we passed each day on the way to the office in Newark. What an ideal place to put a building for small businesses! An ideal incubator-like space where we could offer other small business owners a similar thing to what we were getting at NJIT, plus it has a parking lot. But this was in the days of Sharpe James and the price of this building was astronomical as Newark was under massive redevelopment. It still sits there undeveloped, but the cost of the land makes it unattainable for us. This is one of our biggest regrets.

We also checked out purchasing property like an old house that had adequate parking facilities. It was a good way to include real estate in our holdings. Alas! Nothing compared to what we were paying at the incubator.

All incubators are not equal. Do the legwork to understand what is being offered by each place. Also research the going market rate of office space. One day, we will have to "graduate" from the incubator, but they will have to drag us kicking and screaming!

NUGGET #33 A Board of Advisors is Crucial

By Peggy

I have to credit Sandi with pushing us forward on this one. She kept saying, "we need to form a board…we need to form a board." I thought it was important too, but she really was the gadfly that got us started.

How did we decide to form it and, more important, who did we get to join? We knew it needed to be informal since we were asking people to volunteer their time and knowledge. It had to be a minimal time requirement, so we opted for one meeting per quarter. We also talked to a few other people, mostly fellow business owners, and got their opinion on how they structured and utilized their boards. Again, people were very willing to share their ideas and even recommended potential board members to us. They suggested we get different types of professionals such as accountants, lawyers and senior officers from our target client companies or industries as well as successful entrepreneurs.

From this research, we created a list of potential members. Many were former colleagues or bosses that I had respected and known throughout the years. We then began contacting each person by phone, letter and email. We took many people to lunch to pitch our proposal. In fact, at one of these lunches, we sat next to James Bond (a.k.a. Pierce Brosnan) at the Met Cafe in New York. We took this as a good omen, and we were able to secure our first official board member, Margaret. She was an extremely accomplished executive who had just retired as the former CEO of a business that was started by HSBC and Merrill Lynch. I had worked for her at AT&T and respected her business acumen and her people skills. She was an auspicious start to the board.

Our next board member came to us through luck – that is opportunity meeting preparation. We were on a project for a major Telecom company, and I ran into someone I had known and admired from the 1980s'. We changed jobs and companies, and I lost touch with her, but Katherine was someone I never forgot. She was the first person in the business world that I met who had a successful career, two children, a house, a husband and a nanny. She was a true role model to me and showed me that it was possible to juggle career and family. When we reconnected by chance, it was if we had seen each other only the day before. Another lunch ensued, and I introduced Sandi to her. She was now president of a major division of a Fortune 500 company. We asked her if she would consider being an advisor on our board, and she also agreed. Never underestimate the generosity of people. It still surprises me how many people lent us a hand!

We then recruited two more people to the board – someone I had worked with at Paragon who truly understood the consulting business and a complete stranger. John was referred to us through one of the many helpful business owners we knew. He was an HR director at a major pharmaceutical company and he was also willing to help us out.

After all the board members signed our non-disclosure Agreement, we hosted our first board meeting in Newark and reviewed our strategy, plans and finances with the board. They critiqued our approach and provided us with insightful suggestions. They also became advocates for our company. They referred business to us as well as potential consultants too. It was definitely the right decision and it propelled our business further. Once we told others that we had a board, it also created the perception that we were bigger. Clients, prospects and consultants all viewed it as a sign of a company on the move!

Another benefit of the board was the discipline it fostered within our company. We prepared quarterly updates that we also shared with our team. If you recall, we were initially reticent to share our financials with our core team. But as we sensed people were misunderstanding our margins and revenues, we knew we needed to change. The board meetings and the quarterly updates served as a catalyst that got us to open the books to the team. They helped us to formulate a very specific approach. Once we hired our CFO, we also had him present at these meetings to address all the financial questions.

Now we host quarterly board meetings and quarterly team updates so everyone is on board with where we are headed.

This was another key step in growing the business. I know that the board helped us reach the $1 million mark more quickly and continued to spur our growth. We felt more like the "big leagues" from this initiative. Not only do other people take you more seriously when you make this type of commitment, but you begin to see the dream coming together. I think it was strong reinforcement for us that we were going to do it! It definitely brings that leap of faith alive.

Sandi: Again, having that outside, unbiased view is a tremendous help. I used to look at what the big guys were doing and figured if they used those tools to become successful so could a small company. One of the things that all corporations have is a board. They need some governing body to bring sanity and order to the everyday madness. I joined Boardroom Bound, which is a group that helps to place women and minorities on boards. I didn't join with the intention of being placed on a board myself but more so with the intention of learning what a board should do for a company. I learned that they should be a sounding board as well as help you get business. That's what we needed at the time.

I also attended numerous meetings of NACD in New Jersey. They are a governance body for boards. They had speakers who were on executive boards and a lot of discussions centered on what you need from a board and how to make your board a success. Armed with that knowledge from my research, I was convinced that a board would help us. I also knew that we could not afford to pay anyone who wanted to be on our board, so we should start with people we knew. Peggy knew more people than I did who fit the bill, and we started there.

I suggest to any business person that they gather some kind of advisory body, whether they call it a board or not, but a collection of people who can give sound advice. They should not be people who are going to shoot you down at every turn but people who will challenge you to do better. Even if you don't agree with them all the time, it gives you a view of the world that you would not normally consider. Many of these people have gone through the rough spots in their own careers or businesses, and the advice they gave was practical.

Don't be afraid to "fire" board members if you feel they are not in your best interest. The point is to have someone rooting for you, not against you.

The Company You Should Keep

By Peggy

"Rich Man, Poor Man, Beggar Man, Thief. Doctor, Lawyer, Indian Chief"

American Nursery Rhyme

Assembling a team of competent and trustworthy professionals is crucial to the success of your business. You should develop a relationship with an accountant, a bookkeeper, lawyer(s) and a financial planner. This team will evolve and change as you grow, and you may need to hire and fire several of them before you are satisfied with the right group. We also believe in checks and balances with this team, so no one professional can control all of the finances or legal decisions.

One thing is for sure – they all will differ on their advice. I know we think the law, and especially the tax codes, should give us right and wrong answers, but this is simply not the case. Our lawyer disagrees with our accountants, and the financial planner has a completely different view. It was frustrating at times as we confronted the myriad of business decisions and financial plans that we needed to make. Ultimately, the decisions rested with us, as did the consequences. If we chose the wrong path, tax audits and legal issues would haunt us. That's why it's so important to really research these advisors and ask other business owners, preferably in your industry, for referrals. There is no substitute for experience, and this might be one area where we considered paying a little more for the right person.

Without a doubt the most important advisor for our business is our accountant. Because we had the right person as our accountant early on, he helped us decide the appropriate structure for our business (Corporation, LLC, Partnership, etc.) We chose an LLC. This impacts all future tax filings. As we said in an earlier chapter, homework has to be done.

We outsourced all invoicing to another CPA firm that acts more as our bookkeeper. While he would really like to gain our tax business, we want to maintain a check on his work so we have a separate accountant do our tax work for us. This was a deliberate strategy on our part. Each firm makes recommendations, and we get to hear both sides of the argument on some complex and thorny issues. We pay twice for it, but it is so important to our business, we think it is necessary. Don't forget that we have a CFO who also helps us through these discussions.

C2G actually uses the services of more than one lawyer since there are so many specialties. We have a contract law firm (very expensive – we use them very sparingly) who developed our master consultant contract and reviewed some sticky client ones. We have our trademark attorney who registered our company name and logo and does the renewals. Sometimes we require the services of an employment law specialist, depending on the type of issue that arises. When issues crop up, a team is already in place that knows us and our business and can help us.

Finally, don't forget the financial planner. This is a crucial advisor who helped us decide on retirement plans – something a lot of small business owners don't plan for. Big mistake. Not only is it important for the future but it is a great way to gain tax savings for our business. Initially we used one planner, but decided it wasn't a good fit. We quickly switched to another person that Sandi knew who is very helpful, knowledgeable and practical. There are many plans out there – simple IRAs, 401Ks, profit sharing, so our accountant and planner helped us decide which one makes the most sense for our company.

You cannot know too much on this subject. Get all the advice you possibly can, and be on the lookout for good solid professionals. Spend time here; it will pay off!

Sandi: Small business owners must speak several languages in order to do business well. The languages of financial planning and accounting are two that need interpretation. I think I am fairly savvy at reading through investor reports and plans, but I admit that the 401K package broke me. I called Peggy and asked these questions in rapid succession:

"What does this mean?"

"Where do we sign?"

"Do you understand any of this?"

"Who said we could manage this plan ourselves?"

Have these languages explained to you as they would explain it to a two-year old. If your financial planner can't do that for you, then you know you have the wrong one.

For the lawyer, know that each email will incur a cost. Know that every phone call will incur a cost. As a matter of fact, just by having him, you will incur a cost. But it's necessary. It will cost you even more when you don't use him to check your documents. You can offset the cost by utilizing standard forms or contracts and then customizing them to your needs so the lawyer doesn't have to create the document from scratch but will review it for you.

In regard to all professional services, it's good to have dissention in the ranks. An argument is a good thing that shows us different points of view so we can better understand the consequences of the choices and decisions we make.

NUGGET #35 **Work with Diverse People**

By Sandi

When I walk into corporations today, it literally takes me several minutes to get acclimated to the sounds of all the different accents and languages being spoken. Teams are made up of players in different countries that span different time zones. With this multiculturalism comes understanding or lack thereof. Time zones become a significant factor. You have to catch India before noon EST; you have to have conference calls with Australia late nights or early morning.

As small business owners, we must be willing to work with diverse populations of people, hiring them in our business as well as working with them on the client side. I recently worked on a team where there was a Raj, Rajan, Rajat, Rajeet, and Rajesh. All had thick Indian accents, and across the conference call lines, they all sounded alike. This comment is coming from me, an African-American woman, who used to be the only "diverse" person in the room for years. I learned to constantly ask people to identify themselves before speaking and not take it for granted that I recognize the voice. Many current and potential clients see diversity within our own portfolio of consultants as well as within our client mix.

Diverse people include gay/lesbians, different levels of people (from company presidents who are now working for volunteer organizations to secretaries). Blind and disabled people are also a diverse category, as are veterans, women and ethnic minorities. Consultants 2 Go is a company with an abundance of women consultants. We are ethnically diverse and are capable of working on teams with several different nationalities.

The workforce is rapidly changing and as a small business owner, we have to change with it and reflect the world in our company. I took Spanish starting in public school through college, and the Latin base helps with other languages. I am thinking about taking a third language in order to communicate if we want to become an international business but also to listen better to what is being said; my ears get quickly attuned to the different accents. We also speak to our counterparts in English – it helps to improve theirs. Diversity goes both ways – we have to get other businesses in other countries and not wait for them to do business with us.

Peggy: Today's world demands that you deal with people from all parts of the globe. I regularly sit on teams for my clients that have attendees from the US, Europe, India, Philippines and Canada. To be successful, you need to attract and retain people who represent diverse groups and skills. The only way you can attract them is if you are comfortable with them. Maybe it's because I grew up in New York or that I started the multi-cultural marketing organization at AT&T, but diversity has always been something I have been passionate about, even when corporate America was just starting to "get it." Now it is a business imperative! If you are uncomfortable with diversity, you need to seek opportunities that get you to interact with different types of people to familiarize yourself.

NUGGET #36 The Only Constant is Change

By Peggy

Just when you think you have figured it out, something new comes along that pushes you to reinvent the business – again. For us, it was the financial tsunami of 2008. Fortunately, Sandi and I already know what it's like to work in a small business in hard times since we started the company right after 9/11. We had to do it again when we lost our biggest client in 2005. Then in early 2006, one of our biggest clients changed our payment terms from 15 days to 60 days. We had to restructure then too. Basically, there is no standing still when you own your own business. Adapt or die.

We are facing perhaps our greatest challenge to date – the 2008 economic meltdown and the aftermath. Are we scared? Sure. But we already know what we have to do to win in this climate; we must capitalize on these times. We pivoted our business so that we can sell our services to the newly unemployed and provide outplacement support to our Fortune 500 clients. We have skills that are in great demand now, just for a different set of clients, so we need to refine our marketing plan to hit our targets with the message.

How did we go about it? We had a series of calls and meetings with our team and asked them to think about how we can prosper in these times. What industries and what services should we go after? Then we started to prioritize the list to determine what we needed in place. We met in our Newark office and had a good old fashioned shouting match about what we thought was the right approach. It was healthy and constructive, and now we are making it happen.

Simultaneously, we did not abandon our core business, and we are working our client accounts with vigor. We need to service them better and sell harder in these times and that is what we are doing. At the same time, we rolled out new course curriculum that we developed to target potential new consultants with our classes. We are investigating partnering with several firms to penetrate the healthcare and pharmaceutical industries, which have not been as impacted by this crisis.

What does the future hold? As far as Sandi and I are concerned, there will be a $100 million firm named Consultants 2 Go that prospered and grew exponentially after they launched their self-help series.

Taking risks and living with change is what life is all about. The future can be a bit scary, but with a plan, pluck and persistence, we will prosper!

Sandi: If you don't like change, owning a small business, or any business for that matter, is not for you. It is not for the faint of heart. We knew what we were getting into when we started this business, and we knew we had the personalities and traits to weather the storms of change. I always liked change and in past departments in which I worked, I changed jobs or projects every six months to a year because I liked to work on different things. Peggy and I worked in new industries development because it was a very entrepreneurial area. I see change as good. It shakes up the routine and does a few things: It gives you renewed strength to move forward in a different way; it shows you that what you are doing is correct and can be continued; or it kills you.

NUGGET #37 **Your Financials are Your Best Friend**

By Sandi

I hate QuickBooks. I don't find it to be an intuitive program at all. I'm sure many of you will say "amen" to that. I don't hate spreadsheets though, not if I'm reading them, but I don't want to create them from scratch. Peggy was a finance major and loves the numbers. What we both know from being in corporate is that the numbers tell the tale of good vs. bad, wrong vs. right. All decisions you make for your business will eventually show up in your financials. For that reason alone, *your financials should be your best friend.* You know how many pairs of shoes your best friend has in her closet; you should know how many pairs of shoes you need to sell in order to make your payroll.

I find women are uncomfortable with the financials. Sometimes, I think they feel it is best not to know if they are in a mess, because that will stop their spending. But, equally, there are many women who balance the checkbooks in their families but don't balance the checkbooks in their businesses.

When we decided to apply for the Make Mine a Million $ Business award in 2005, we took a look at our financials and knew right away that we were not in a position to present those financials to anyone. Not that we were unprofitable, but we needed to invest time to clean up our books and to have our financials truly reflect how much we had grown year over year. In 2006, with clean financials (no longer on an Excel spreadsheet), we applied and won the award. We were able to clearly show that we had double-digit growth each year since 2002 when we started our business. The good thing about the Make Mine a Million program is it didn't stop there. As a participating awardee, you must send your financials to Count Me In's CFO. Libby scrutinized it and then gave us suggestions or reached out to us if she felt we were going to be in trouble. We were comfortable with the numbers but did not have the expertise to give it the in-depth analysis that was needed.

We took a QuickBooks class. We pretty much bartered for the class with a Women's Business Center. We wanted to be able to check each day to see how we're doing. Our eyes glazed over but out of that Peggy became the QuickBooks guru.

We hired an accounting firm. It was a hard decision, financially, but we needed to take back some of the hours that we spent balancing our books. We interviewed several individuals and companies with whom we wanted to feel a level of comfort if they were going to, figuratively, take our books into their hands. We still spend time reviewing the books, but we don't have to do all the dreaded data entry. And as much as I hate QuickBooks, I do recognize that it is a Godsend. Balance sheets, income and cash flow statements magically appear at the click of a button. You can review your books on a cash basis and then switch to an accrual basis.

Hiring a CFO was the best money we ever spent. We wanted additional reporting that neither our accountant nor Peggy and I were equipped to put together. We needed expertise on our financials. Who is responsible for bringing in the most sales? The sales report can be made to look bloated but the receivables and payables do not lie. He works part-time and is the ex-CFO of a major Fortune 500 corporation. What a catch!

At our quarterly review meetings, we make projections on how much in sales we project, what expenses needs to be cut, how many hours each person can work for that month, etc. Previously, our team knew how much in sales they were bringing in but they didn't have the other side of the financials to see how much was going out. Once we created transparency with our financials, they became even better team players. Each person knew exactly how much they needed to bring in and how it would be spent. This knowledge made them extremely competitive with each other. It also forced the sales team to push for higher margins, forced our recruiter to ensure we get great people on our team as it is costly to remove a consultant when they are on a project, and forced the management to create a realistic, achievable strategy that can help our company move forward.

All those great outcomes came from knowing our financials. We will continue to share our books with our team in the hopes that they will feel some sense of ownership for their roles in the business.

Peggy: You won't be in business long if you don't understand the numbers...especially cash flow! When you run a business, you need to understand how long it takes you to collect from your customers and when you need to pay your suppliers. I will tell you that I really watch our receivables, and I don't have any problems asking a customer for money owed. In the beginning, it felt a little awkward, but now I know how important it is. I usually like to get some payment up front when I can or start the billing cycle immediately once we start. Many large companies have a process for paying you, and you need to understand it and comply with all their paperwork requirements to get paid. The sooner you figure out this process, the speedier you will be paid.

Finally, I always try to get paid electronically if possible; it almost negates collections. Typically, if they have electronic payment as an option, all it requires is that you provide them with your bank account number and bank routing number (the other numbers located at the bottom of your check). Many companies actually prefer to pay electronically as it is more efficient...plus you won't get the dreaded "the check is in the mail."

NUGGET #38 Your CFO is Your Next Best Friend

By Peggy

Sometimes you have to go with your gut when opportunity knocks. Last year, our board member, Katherine, shared with us the resume of one of her former colleagues, Doug. He was the recently retired CFO for a $10 billion company. He was looking to do some consulting on a part-time basis in his new life. While she presented his resume as someone we might want to talk to as a potential consultant, we had other plans. When Sandi and I were handed his resume, we immediately wanted to talk to him. While we had an accountant and bookkeeper, we really needed someone to look at our business and provide a strategic assessment – someone who could help us actively take the company to the next level and design a blueprint for future success.

It was one of the best decisions we made thus far! We didn't sit around and wait to offer Doug the position. Once I spoke with him, I told Sandi that I thought he was exactly what we needed. She concurred and we moved quickly. He wanted to work part time so this was a great fit for us. We were able to negotiate a deal with him that met our budget and his needs.

We were delighted when he said yes. *We have found him to be a great asset to the organization.* He immediately got started evaluating our business. Within a month, he had done a complete analysis of our business and was able to set up metrics and scorecards that were extremely helpful. We were able to assess our performance in "real time" and make better and timely decisions. In addition, his experience was invaluable with the rest of the team. Before his arrival, they debated with us about some of the things we were asking of them to run our business such as reports we required from them. Once Doug started asking for the information, it somehow stopped all the back and forth. His experience and authority stopped the debates and got us focused and on track. When he reviewed the numbers, they didn't challenge him as they had challenged us in the past. I think his presence created a new dynamic within the company that helped create a culture that would take us to the next level.

Probably one of the biggest benefits of having a CFO is the credibility it gives you with clients. Suddenly they view your small business in a new light. People start to perceive you as a much bigger company. This is especially important with Fortune 500 companies, as they are our principal clients. These companies want to know that you are able to handle a large company and that you have the appropriate resources. Doug provided that image with them. He also reached out to his former colleagues on our behalf. This proved invaluable as well. He was able to open doors for us to the "C" Suite that we had difficulty entering.

Sandi: Other people we knew had CFOs and we thought that it must be an expensive venture for them to take on. Some of those people could not articulate the difference between their CFO and their bookkeeper so at one point, I thought we were going in the right direction with a bookkeeper and two accountants but I knew the strategic guidance was missing in terms of our financials. Peggy and I are good at analytics, and yes, Peggy was a finance major, but it most definitely lends a whole new perspective when you have someone who is using their knowledge of how a Fortune 500 company operates vs. our middle-management viewpoint.

We don't have to have our CFO on staff; this position is outsourced and is part-time. As a matter of fact, we could not have afforded to pay a tenured CFO a salary. There are companies who now have consultants for just the "C" suite. Use them.

NUGGET #39 Checks and Balances in Your Business

By Sandi

As I previously stated, I don't like QuickBooks, so Peggy does all the double-checking of the accounts. By the time I see the books, it's all cleaned up. My third eye is helpful because I can spot things that look out of line but the reality is by the time I see it, I'm actually more like a fifth eye.

When the entry work got too tedious and we were spending too much time doing the books, we hired a bookkeeping firm to do all entries, submit invoices and follow up on late payments. Second best money we ever spent. Our books are a little complicated for a simple consulting company. It is based on the client set-up; for some companies, we are subcontractors, while we are direct vendors with most of them. Our records have to be kept accordingly.

We hired one of the companies in the incubator to assist with our books. During the week, our bookkeeper does all the entries. On the weekend, Peggy reviews the entries to make sure they are correct. She makes corrections, and prints and signs the checks. She also puts the check in the mail.

After that first set of books is done, we need customized spreadsheets for our CFO. Our business analyst takes the QuickBooks spreadsheets and reorganizes them into more detail that is not produced by a canned application. Our CFO gets into a level of granularity that only a CFO can. This gives us another chance to sync up the accounts. Sometimes expenses are recorded in the wrong category and, therefore, look inflated. The category immediately looks out of pattern.

Our first accountant, Ed, is Peggy's older brother. Ed is an amazing accountant. One of our board members suggested that we also get an accountant who can help us structure ourselves for sale. It was a good idea. It also gave us two accountants to check each other. This way, we knew that our financial decision was well thought out. It was an expensive proposition, and we did not get as much out of it as we would have liked, but once again, both accountants bounced ideas off of us and we, in turn, bounced off them.

My financial advisor, George, also weighs in on 401K plans vs. Ed's financial planner. When we get the same answer from both of them, we know we are on the right track.

We are back with Ed as our accountant but, from time-to-time it makes sense to get another opinion. It keeps everyone sharp and on our toes. I feel a lot more confident with the decisions we make when we have several people giving the same advice. We still take everything into consideration and make our own decisions in the end, but these decisions have a base and we have a particular comfort level with them. It can get expensive to have more than one person checking your books but you can do it for a short period of time and not on an ongoing basis.

Peggy: Ask three different experts, expect three different answers. That's why I always like to get several opinions if possible. Laws, taxes and regulations are complicated and not necessarily designed for the small business. You don't want to get yourself into trouble or have financial problems because you didn't do your due diligence. Don't shortchange yourself in this area. This is where the real issues can come in and sabotage a business.

NUGGET #40 The Tax Man Cometh!

By Peggy

No matter how much we thought we knew about finances, taxes and money management, this is one area that we can never know enough about. We definitely got surprised with our tax bill.

How did this happen? In 2006, we had a tremendous year. Our revenues grew by approximately 300% on an accrual basis (booked the income when it was earned rather than when the payment was actually received). This was the year that we hit the million dollar mark with the business. Much of the revenue came through in the last half of the year. We were feeling like we had finally gotten to the next level, and we were very proud. Most women-owned businesses never reach this milestone, and we were with the 3% who do.

What we didn't really pay attention to was that our business paid its taxes on a cash basis. A significant portion of the actual payments from our clients came in early 2007. While we paid our correct amount in 2006, we didn't understand or appreciate the impact that the cash flowing in the first quarter of 2007 would do to us when we had to pay our 2007 taxes. We had another good year. We grew by 40% in '07 and reached the $1.4 million mark. However, that was on an actual cash basis as opposed to an accrual basis; we increased our revenue by 80% in 2007 and went into a new tax bracket as well. So, our estimated taxes were too low, and when we finally had everything trued up by our accountants, we got a very nasty surprise.

We had to pay a much larger bill than we estimated and were, therefore, hit with additional penalties. In addition, our estimated taxes in 2008 needed to be increased significantly so we wouldn't have the same situation again. This really depleted our cash reserves but we had no choice because delaying these payments would only cost us more.

What did we decide to do as a result of this? We ensured our CFO helped us to better understand our business in real time. We also educated ourselves on our options for reducing our taxes – whether it was taking the maximum allowable deductions, understanding various tax-free savings plans like Simple IRAs or 401Ks for the company or realizing payments to vendors in the appropriate tax year.

If we had to do it over again, I know Sandi and I would have done a better job of understanding the implications of these increases in revenue crossing calendar years. We also would have made different pricing decisions, because our true costs were higher than we estimated since our taxes were greater than we thought. We certainly should have gotten our accountant more involved earlier on, but we didn't in order to save time and money. In the end, it cost us more since it ate up a lot of our reserves that we could have invested in the business.

I wish I had taken a course on small business taxation when we first considered establishing the business. I think it would have helped me understand the pitfalls and mistakes many businesses make and would have given me a better understanding of what we needed to do. While we did surround ourselves with some knowledgeable people, and we were able to quickly rectify the situation, with a little knowledge, we would have been better prepared and done a better job estimating our costs in 2007.

I can't tell you how many small business owners whom I've met in the last seven years who really screwed up in this area. They wound up owing so much in taxes that it forced them to go out of business. They are still working through tax liens and other problems because they never realized the trouble you can get into if you don't set it up correctly. This is one area where everyone should get professional advice, and the sooner the better!

Sandi: I'm still reeling from the taxes we had to pay. Yes, I do understand why we are paying this much in taxes…now! I'm definitely taking more interest in money mathematics. We also need to think about estate planning as well, but, geez, first I would like to get an estate for which to plan!

Even if you get an accountant, a bookkeeper and a CFO, you still need to get a basic understanding of what needs to be done in regards to keeping the books. Involve the accountant and others right at the start and do not wait until you are making money to do so. Once you're making money without their involvement, you might have to hand over most of it to Uncle Sam.

NUGGET #41 You're the Boss – the Buck Stops with You

By Sandi

Every day decisions have to be made. Make that every 10 minutes, actually. When we had a job, we deferred some of those decisions and let our boss make them for us. They told us when they needed something, told us how they wanted it and we gave it to them. They told us who will be in the audience for a presentation. They knew what health insurance is being offered to employees. What about investing in a Simple IRA or 401K? As a business owner, we are the ones giving directions! We are the ones to whom our team turns for the strategy, to be told what to do.

Layoff decisions can be made by senior management on a job. We are now the senior management. Someone else was in charge of appraisals; now, we have to give appraisals to our team (in a timely manner). We get to give the great feedback as well as making sure the negative ones are constructive. We have to fire the lazy guy instead of letting him hang himself over time. We recently had to make some of these tough calls as we had to reduce our labor pool as well as reduce hours with the consultants who do our sales, recruiting and office management. We did this in an effort to keep people working but if revenues were not being generated – through no fault of their own but due to economic shifts – we could not pay them. As we told those consultants, we had to be honest that we would expect more out of them while cutting their hours. We hope they saw that we were trying to ensure that everyone kept their assignments while, at the same time, making the company viable for a longer period of time. Because the buck stopped with us, we were the ones looking people in the faces to deliver these messages.

During this time of economic upheaval, we had to figure out the team we would keep in a worst-case scenario. Then if it got worse, who would be the last man standing with us? How comfortable were we with our own decisions? Were we making the right choices? They were all extremely difficult decisions because we really liked our team, and we worked well together. But when we couldn't pay everyone, then someone had to go.

When our clients gave us feedback on our consultants, we had to deliver it to them. If we were not the ones doing the actual delivery, we first had to discuss it with the messenger to ensure that the feedback was understood. If action needed to be taken on specific topics, then we had to give recommendations on how to get it done. Recently, we were told by a client that we needed to ensure that our consultants had great Microsoft Office skills. It was new feedback for us and we had to deliver this to consultants who were at the higher end of the rate spectrum. These are consultants who have always had an associate or administrative assistant to do their clean-up work. Now that they were on the other side of the table, they needed to learn how to do it themselves. We were able to investigate where they could get classes and created new classes for them when there were none. Having the buck stop with us meant responsibility also began with us.

Should we hoard away money for next year or should we spend money on heavy marketing now? We are a marketing company and we certainly advocated marketing in a down economy. But could we walk the talk without revenues?

We know that when we make a decision to take on a client, sometimes it is against the good advice of our core team, but we are the bosses. One recent case was where we emphatically decided we were not going to put a lot of time into small companies (one to five people); and these companies must generate a certain revenue threshold to make the opportunity feasible for us. Yet, when Victoria called to say that she had a project on which she wanted us to work, we didn't hesitate in scoping it out, putting together a proposal, and getting a consultant to work on her project. We had clearly said to our team that this is not a market that we would pursue. We had previous bad experiences with smaller businesses but the lure of money snared us. We wasted a lot of time and, therefore, money, trying to bring this project to fruition…yet it was fruitless. Why didn't we learn from our past mistakes? Because we're the bosses and sometimes your team is just afraid to say no to you. And we needed to listen to ourselves more.

Still we kept devising ways to work with smaller businesses because we got help when we need it. What kept us honest was that we clearly articulated our strategy for the year. Every time we wanted to give someone a chance, our team brought up the strategy, and it was enough to give us pause.

A lot of the critical thinking that took place was out of sight of our staff and team. They usually saw the final outcome. We have learned to pull our team into the decision-making process. We now understand that they have a stake in the business as well and will be more vested if we include them.

At the end of the day, the last call is always ours. But at least we can turn to our board to help with tough decisions before we speak to our costly lawyer or accountants.

We made these decisions with confidence knowing that we were not invincible. We will make a lot more mistakes (have learnings) than we will be right on point. We try not to be too hard on ourselves. And we are not afraid to say "we made a mistake." After all, we are the bosses!

Peggy: It's important to make decisions and move quickly if you want to be successful. One thing I have learned is not to beat myself up when decisions turn out badly. You are required by the very nature of the pace of business to act and move swiftly, so there will be times that things go wrong. Learn from them so you don't repeat them, but don't dwell on them – you will waste your valuable energy on a fruitless exercise.

NUGGET #42 Kiss 4 Weeks of Vacation Goodbye

By Sandi

We said we wanted to start our own businesses because we would have more time; we could work when we wanted to, we would spend more time with our family and friends, we would travel to places that we previously had no time to go. Guess what? Having a small business keeps me glued to my computer from 6 a.m. in the morning straight back to 3 a.m. the next morning…and then I do it all over again.

I am a Jack (or Jacqueline) of all trades. Some people have been able to take four weeks of vacation, but I must say that, overall, in the first few years of business, neither Peggy nor I left our business behind. Taking a few days off proved to be a major challenge, much less an entire week. Time off would have been much easier if we had a trained staff; however, as a two-woman shop, when our clients needed something we couldn't tell them to wait while we basked in the sun.

Having a business partner makes a difference. For the first time in seven years, we have an overlap in vacation time. We planned vacations around school schedules so there were a limited number of times that we could take. I've given up a summer vacation because I was on a short-term project that lasted from June to September.

Many people gave me great advice about ending my day at a particular time, and turning off my computer…it didn't work for me then, and doesn't work for me now. If I am writing a proposal that is due the next day, or if I am waiting on a critical email, am I not going to keep on my computer? What would I say to my client? That it was 5 p.m. and I had to go?

Because C2G assignments are largely in three-month increments, if we know ahead of schedule that we or our consultants will be out for one of those weeks, we tell our client in advance. Sometimes, it's a deal breaker if they will be at a critical juncture in the project and the consultant will be needed. We either give them another person or have someone experienced to cover for them.

I recall spending hundreds of dollars on email connectivity while I cruised the Caribbean. I was on a project where I had to constantly respond to emails and have input. I checked in twice per day and told my client what time to expect a response. The fact is as a business owner, being on a cruise ship did not prevent me from responding to my client when she needed my help.

My family feels that my laptop is my second child. We are joined at the hip. I rarely leave home without it. If I don't have my laptop, I have a flash drive of every document that is on my drive so that I can use it on someone else's computer in a pinch. In this regard, having a Blackberry is a wonderful thing – I can still communicate with my team or client, but the drawback is that I really can't comfortably work on large documents like financial spreadsheets that are attachments. Is a vacation with my laptop still a vacation? I say yes! My family still enjoy themselves (sometimes without me) but I feel I fulfilled my agreement to bring them someplace wonderful.

Seven years into this, I have learned to build in at least two weeks where I have very little check-in with the office or my business partner. I do bring my Blackberry but I've learned to leave my computer behind. We now have a shared drive where we keep critical documents that everyone has access to, so I don't feel that I am the only person on earth with a particular document that is needed.

The word "sick" is literally a four-letter word in my vocabulary. You will not sneeze on me, I can function on two hours or less of sleep, I will get up and work from home when I have the flu (taking doses of medication in between), I will try to do my exercises more diligently because I can't afford to be sick (or the cost of my medical insurance co-pay).

Nugget #42 Kiss 4 Weeks of Vacation Goodbye

I am writing this chapter on a Sunday at noon because I am on a deadline for this book. I wrote yesterday before I went to a gala affair. The job doesn't stop for me, and I have to slowly learn to stop for the job.

There is a woman in my Make Mine a Million group who has several children and runs a successful million-dollar business in a man's world. She reads every book that comes out, she takes vacations trekking across the country in a shoe (RV, that is) with every child in tow. I aspire to be her. I asked Theresa how she does it and, indeed, she has a personal assistant, a nanny and a cleaning lady! That's the trick. We should all aspire to be her because she shows that it can be done. I just don't know how many of us will reach our aspirations. I will need an amazing amount of coordination and organization to accomplish that. Perhaps when I'm rich enough, I'll just hire other people to plan my vacation, clean my house and free up my time so that I, too, can actually go on the vacation.

Peggy: Sandi is right; I work more than ever. But I also enjoy work more than ever. And I get to do it on my terms, which gives me an incredible sense of empowerment and accomplishment! I always tell people that owning my business has allowed me to lead a "blended life." (Note – not balanced, but blended). I am able to work with my clients in the morning then stop and pick up my daughter from school, handle a conference call and then take her to ballet. Fix dinner and then back to my computer for a few hours. Unlike Sandi, I do need sleep! I also don't beat myself up anymore either. Some days, the company does win and some days my family does. This is life – no perfect balance but one that constantly needs juggling.

NUGGET #43 **Read About Your Industry**

By Sandi

It is imperative that we know what is happening in our industries. It is a difficult and onerous task to read all the trade publications, keep up with emails and attend trade events. But we must find time and schedule it into our strategic plan. This also helps us to track the newest trends in the industry. We know when major political decisions will impact our business and are better able to prepare for it. Things we learned from reading:

1. We are a women-owned certified business. Policies regarding small business, women-owned businesses, certifications impact us. We were frantically completing RFP's for small business and women-owned business set-asides in New Jersey. Once we read that the state was eliminating set-asides, it helped us to make a strategic decision to move away from that type of business and the government sector.

2. The most recent literature was regarding the economic impact on our clients in the financial services industry. We could not possibly know the extent of what was going on with individual companies until we started reading about it in daily publications.

    a. There was an increase in number of articles regarding finance charges, irate customers in the credit card industry and lawsuits against our clients.

    b   Our client's winning of a major class action suit meant they would be able to hire more consultants to reinstate several projects that were put on hold.

c. The concerns regarding the financial standing of our clients in the banking industry alerted us that contracts might be canceled and payments would be getting slower. We were able to speak to our consultants to give them a heads-up on the state of the business and to listen to the language of executives that corroborated our thinking – we especially listened for what was not said vs. what was said. Because of that, we were able to start tightening our own belts in anticipation for a worst-case scenario if we lost our contracts.

3. What are the trends going on in Marketing? Online subscriptions to Advertising Age, New York Times, NJ Biz and marketing newsletters let us know that social media is becoming extremely popular in marketing to the younger generation. Marketing in the recent presidential elections confirmed our suspicions. Receiving emails from candidates, seeing the reports on social media in magazines confirmed what we needed to do. We knew our clients would be following suit with utilizing this new media. As our company has all tenured, experienced consultants who do not necessarily have that skill set, we were able to start recruiting for those skills that we traditionally do not have in our stable. We also set out to acquire those skills ourselves.

4. What are our competitors doing? Did they win an award or a new client? Where are they finding new business? Who are our clients using, if not us? Hopefully, our competitors are reading about us as well.

Our business crosses industries. C2G is in the marketing, analytics and consulting industries, as well as financial services, telecom and insurance. We also have some peripheral industries in which we play. There are not enough hours in the day to read up on all these things, but we must keep up.

I recently purchased an audio book. I listened to it in my car and made use of the driving time. I also take a magazine with me to the beauty parlor and the doctor – one trick is to take out the article if you need it and leave the magazine in the office so that someone else can gain something from it instead of placing it in the recycle bin. The airplane and the train are also great places to catch up on reading.

Peggy: I am a voracious reader. I have a magazine or book with me at all times. It is also my way of relaxing. However, to keep abreast of industry trends, I subscribe to several online services that send me news alerts about daily events and breaking stories. I have several general ones (New York Times, Crain's NY), and then two industry-specific ones that keep me posted about the latest news in telecommunications and financial services. I am constantly scouring different sites and blogs to keep up with the latest views and maintain a pulse on the general climate of the times. Sandi gets Advertising Age for marketing news and NJ Biz for local small business happenings.

NUGGET #44 Our Million-Dollar Work-from-Home Hobby

By Sandi

During our corporate days, we yearned to have the ability to work from home. We wanted to be able to take our children to school, look in on the baby on our breaks, or take our parents to the doctor. Corporate created flexible work arrangements but we never really worked full-time from home, perhaps on Fridays. Somehow, our families thought when we were home on Fridays that was the greatest thing because they knew from Monday through Thursday we were not available to them.

After being laid off, we were home for almost a year before we started thinking about the business. We were doing exactly what we wanted to do. When we started out, it was just Peggy and me so we did not have the need for an office. We went onsite to the client if they needed us. We could enjoy the best of both worlds.

The first year was really spent setting up the business. On the family side, we still made the ballet lessons and responded to the last-minute phone calls for bringing someone home to dinner or needing to be dropped someplace obscure – and we made all those schedule changes quite easily without thinking about them.

One day, that changed. Revenues were easily stretching into six figures. At that time, we started to get irritated at these last-minute family phone calls. We asked our families to make sure we have their schedules ahead of time, but quite frankly, they didn't understand why as we were home all day. Why can't we pick up the phone to speak to them? Why can't we pick them up from their friend's home at 3:30 p.m. – you're only speaking on the phone all day (conference calls count as just speaking on the phone). Significant others started to be annoyed when they told us they had to work late and can't we make the trek across town to pick up the children. Yes, they know it's their turn, but it's not like we're not home.

Funny how that changes when you get an office space that you visit every day. Now, we don't have a hobby any longer, we have a *real job*! Peggy's husband, Robert, used to come in whistling while she was on conference calls. My mother would ask me to hold on for a minute so she could tell me about the cat's latest escapade.

Honestly, I don't think the perception changed until after Robert started to work from home. Then he understood having someone else in the same room printing a countless number of presentations while he had to speak on the phone. My mother started to get it when she saw the newspaper articles and Money magazine cover; plus the bills were getting paid.

Family is going to be just that – family. They are there to thwart and test us at every turn. We developed superior organization skills, we learned how to scream at them with our eyes, we learned to buy a phone with a mute button and took it all in stride and continued to execute. Malcolm Gladwell says everything has a tipping point. What was our family's tipping point in realizing that we have a business? Perhaps for my family, it was the fact that I started to give little cues such as closing the door and putting up a sign on the door saying "Woman at Work." I also stopped for about 30 minutes when they came home, to speak to them and catch up on their day so that they didn't feel neglected. We devised our own methods to work around our families until they came to their senses.

Peggy: Learning to work while at home is definitely an art form. My husband is an incurable whistler. My son Robbie (now at college) was a typical little boy who could not contain himself when he had something to share or ask me. He just would run into the office. So, I had to train myself and my family how to act when I was working. My children both began to write me notes when they needed to ask me something right away. If it was a particularly important call, I would close the door and then suddenly notes would be sent underneath. My husband also tried to be more cognizant of his whistling when I was on a conference call, and he got to know my gestures if there were momentary lapses. The key here is to lay some ground rules with your family so that you create an environment that's conducive to work but still maintains a good relationship with your family members.

NUGGET #45 **Telecommuting**

By Sandi

Working from home is a wonderful thing. We can work in our pajamas and big bunny slippers without washing our faces or brushing our teeth. And many times we do just that.

What I love about telecommuting is that it can be an extremely productive way to work. The opposite is also true. Some people like to have an office to go to because if they don't see other people to hold them accountable, they will not get a single thing done. We like to have a choice so there are days when we work from home and, when we need to get together and sing Kum Ba Yah, we go into the office.

Pro:

The trip to Newark, NJ, from Brooklyn, NY, is approximately 33 miles each way. That is in miles, not time. When I travel in off hours (after 9 a.m.), it takes 40 minutes. Most of the times, if I go to the office during "regular" hours (leaving home by 7:30 a.m.), it can take up to 1.5 hours. When there is inclement weather, add another half hour. I've turned around and gone back home because the traffic was so horrible. This is not counting about $20 in tolls and another half tank of gas.

When I work from home, I avoid all the noise, bustle and costs. I can get up at the same time (around 6 a.m.) and start to work. I review and complete documents and proposals that have to go out for the day and get it to my client by the time they get in to work. I can start conference calls much earlier, which is especially useful in different time zones. Using a service like FreeConference.com really helps because we can have numerous people on one phone call. Other great technology that enables working from home is having hi-speed internet to download files as well as having a fax machine or eFax; a good color printer is also a must; and having a backup hard drive is definite.

By allowing our team to work from home, we also save quite a bit of these expenses. We do not have to open our offices every day because there is no need. Of course, our home bills slightly increased but a portion of that can be written off to our business.

In a gas shortage environment, it helps to save gas too, so the impact on the pollution will certainly be a positive one. Additionally, it is an opportunity to retain a team member. Research shows that people who telecommute are much more loyal to their organizations – this is a perk that they do not want to give up. Training a new person is expensive to a small business and turnover only costs us more.

An additional benefit is there is no one dropping by my desk to interrupt me. I am able to work for prolonged periods of time without interruption and am usually more productive as a result.

Con:

Telecommuting is not for people who are only team players. Even though it is a team effort to keep this business running, some people crave the face to face contact and simply relate better in person. They feed off other people's energy and shut down when they don't have that. One of our salespeople preferred the camaraderie of people to working alone. She wanted to see people every day and felt she was just closeted at home all day. We all know there is a level of mixing business with home duties and C2G is extremely tolerant of the flexibility that working with us gives our consultants; however, they have to recognize that this is still a business, and the needs and demands of the business comes first. They cannot schedule our clients around their children's kindergarten pick-up hours – find a babysitter who can do that. She never fully learned how to do that.

Also, speaking of babysitters, we require our consultants who have young children and work from home to have someone take care of their young children while they work. It is unprofessional to have children screaming during a client call or put a client on hold to sign for packages from the delivery person.

When our clients know we work from home, they automatically feel we are accessible to them on a 24-hour basis. We get emails that expect an answer at 1 a.m. or 6 a.m., or 5 p.m. – all requesting a quick response.

That said, we make it work. We attempt to set office hours when we work from home. Let both our office and families know our hours so they can both manage expectations. I have a cue to my family that when my door is closed, they cannot interrupt. It's perfectly OK if I want to come out and join them in an activity but they should not expect that will happen daily.

I started to enforce small things like my mother not shouting up the stairs to tell me that she's home or, worse yet, announcing it for my entire conference call to hear over the intercom. When Lauren comes home now, she automatically assumes that I am working if she brings friends home. She doesn't come in with a bang anymore.

Another thing that I'm learning (and I'm poor at it) is to break up the monotony and stop working at particular times to eat, drink water and run errands. I tend to work straight through the day and forget about eating. Then I eat late at night and that weight gain is taking its toll. I am practicing to do everything like I am at the office. It's not easy but it's worth the effort.

As for my clients, I let them know that I will always get back to them within 24 hours of their email or call – even if I respond right away. Sometimes I force myself not to respond immediately as, again, I am setting expectations that I might not be able to meet later.

Peggy: I really enjoy the flexibility that telecommuting brings. I can work where and when I like. I realized that certain tasks (like writing this book) require me to move out of the home office and down to a more creative spot in the house – like my kitchen table (with a view to my wooded backyard) or deck. If I stay at my desk, I start doing other non-essential tasks that distract me from the job at hand. However, I do have a wireless router, so I can receive emails and print from any room in my house. This keeps me abreast of any urgent matters.

When you telecommute you need to understand where and how you work. You really have to do a self assessment to find out what tasks you can do well in certain environments and what tasks need to be done in other locations. I couldn't have written this book in my office. My office has far too many distractions with constant reminders of all the daily chores I need to complete to allow me to think creatively. I need an environment that is more tranquil that allows my "juices" to flow for me to be able to imagine and create new materials. The key to working at home is to know thyself and figure out what works best for you!

NUGGET #46 **You are Stronger than You Think**

By Sandi

There is no better time for our strength to float to the surface than when business is bad or when a project is not going according to plan. We usually say "if that happens to us, we won't know what we would do." The truth is when it comes right down to it, we are a lot stronger than we think we are. When our business is in jeopardy, we rise to the occasion to defend it similar to a tiger defending its cub.

There were times when family, friends and colleagues asked, "Why don't you throw in the towel and go back to a real job?!" And frankly, sometimes it took a lot of resolve not to listen to them. We became creative, we cut costs that we previously thought we could not live without, and we let people go whom we thought were indispensable.

In the first year of our company, it was hard for us to ask our clients for business. We wrongly thought if we worked hard, it would come to us. After analyzing that other consulting companies were getting projects, we found it much easier to ask for business. It's still not easy, mind you. But it is certainly easier and has become a part of how we speak. Recently, we went into a client with whom we have been trying to crack the code on what it takes to place more than one consultant at a time. When they told us that they already use a consulting company and that the owner of the consulting company was the neighbor of the client, it did not deter us. We were able to point out why we are different (we're in the local area whereas the other company is regional); we knew we had to fight to even be considered. In the end, the client felt that we could be more viable because we can give them consultants who can be onsite when needed. Seven years ago, we would have been put off by that acknowledgment. Now, we are able to stand toe to toe with any competitor, large or small.

We are able to give negative feedback in a candid manner that is not off-putting. Sometimes we just have to tell our consultants something that they don't want to hear. We have developed a backbone in being clear as to whether or not they are fulfilling our requirements on a project.

Women are generally more sentimental than men when it comes to making tough decisions. But when we need to, we will make them. We kept giving one particular consultant numerous chances to come up to speed even though she was not being productive, because we really liked her. But one day, we realized that we had to make this hard decision that would not be to the consultant's liking, but it's strictly business…and we still hope we can be civil to each other if we run into each other in a dark alley.

Peggy: It's funny, but when things go bad, that's when Sandi and I really jump into action. We have evolved over the seven years. We are less intimidated by bigger companies or big bosses. We have learned that we can handle the most difficult situation and still maintain our integrity. We are now more likely to let someone know that they are not meeting our expectations in a shorter time frame. We have learned that waiting will not make the situation go away or get easier. We have learned that the thought of doing it and anticipating outcomes are actually worse then the actual task.

NUGGET #47 **The World of Certification**

By Sandi

We were seduced into the world of certification. Certification, in this case, refers to the confirmation that Peggy and I are women, that I am not Caucasian and neither of us are veterans. This confirmation is provided by external parties. The two most nationally known certifying agencies are the National Minority Supplier Development Council (NMSDC), which tells the world that I'm a minority of some kind, and the Women's Business Enterprise National Council (WBENC) which declares that Peggy and I are women. I confess that I have always been suspicious of the latter as no one has ever asked me to undress, see my birth certificate or asked my mother. Additionally, all federal, state and city agencies have their own certification processes. Once you receive your certificate, you then must register into every individual corporation's database, providing a copy of your certificate.

Everyone told us that as women and minority business owners, doors would be opened to us – widely. That is not quite how the story goes. I honestly can say that we've knowingly only received one piece of very small business because we are a women/minority-owned company. We were immensely qualified for this gig, but we would not have been chosen otherwise.

The first diversity event that we attended was at the New York/New Jersey Minority Supplier Development Council. We were impressed, as everyone who was anyone in politics in New Jersey was there. We remembered the now indicted politician speaking about everyone having to "be at the table" in order to share in the food. He was later sent to jail because he was eating too much under the table.

Here are our issues with certification:

a. City, state, federal – Everyone has their own idea of what certification entails. New York City has a tome that you have to complete and get notarized. Empire State (New York State) has a similar tome but when we started out with certification, neither entity accepted the other. You had to complete these two documents with the same information, placed strategically in different places so that you couldn't just copy it. Some entities, both government and corporate, now have joint certifications. After taking a look at federal, we just decided that it was not worth all the aggravation that we had to go through. Perhaps we'll take another look now that the government is doling out money!

b. Disabled and veterans – Neither of us qualify for these sectors. It can definitely be an advantage if we were going into a military or government area. I'm sure marketing people for the Armed Services have an easier time getting in because they are ex-military. Neither Peggy nor I can claim any disabilities. Personally, I think that wearing glasses is a major disability but it doesn't count.

c. Women and minority-owned businesses – Similar to government, every corporation has its own certification process that needs to be completed. Now, most corporations outsource this work and have an online site to visit, but years ago, it was all paper-based. Corporations accept either the NMSDC (minority) or WBENC (women) certification as proof. It would be immensely easier if those agencies were the only ones responsible for certification and maintain a database that corporations can access. However, each certifying agency is a business and charges approximately $100 for certification fees.

We decided to stop pursuing government contracts because it was taking too much time to respond to the Request for Proposals (RFPs). It would take both Peggy and me at least two weeks to prepare a response. This was in addition to the time spent by our partners and consultants who were bidding jointly with us on these projects. All of this with no pay and a huge expenditure of time.

One time, we responded to a local municipal RFP that wanted marketing, a rare thing. After pulling together our colleagues to formulate the proposal, we were told we were finalists. This entailed additional work, which included giving actual copies of our ad. We were uncomfortable with doing so but knew we had to do it to be given access to present. After two hours of questioning – at which they were really excited at the ideas we presented – they told us they would get back to us.

A few weeks later, we were told that none of the respondents or finalists was able to give them what they needed and the RFP was going to be withdrawn. Later, we saw our work prominently displayed in an ad campaign for the same service that was previously advertised. No new RFP was given. We were devastated and started down the path to find out what happened and how our ideas and concepts were put into use without us getting payment or acknowledgement for it.

We wrote letters to the Mayor and his staff complaining of the injustice that was done to a small business. The response we received, as all others have, is that these ideas and concepts were already in the works. We decided then that we would not respond to any more RFPs.

We hired a lobbyist to open doors for us in New York City. We attended numerous meetings with top council members at the time. However, none of these meetings proved fruitful, as they had already established a familiarity with another company. We did not get any assignments. Those meetings helped us to solidify our decision not to enter that sector.

There are small businesses that work, successfully, in the government sector that must be certified; I've met few of them. A company can also get business from corporate certifications as corporations, too, must meet a diversity threshold; and they try to ensure that all boxes are checked with their vendor relationships, meaning they give some key minorities or women's businesses a contract to satisfy their survey and PR needs.

Determine if your business will benefit from certification. We still certify with selected entities. It benefits us as a woman-owned and minority business in case a client asks for it. What certification says to me is that you have passed a strict set of criteria that gives you instant credibility, because of all the financial paperwork that you must provide. What it doesn't say is that you are unlikely to get business because of it.

Peggy: We spent a lot of time in the beginning getting certified. Then we had a lot of agency people tell us that we should go for government contracts. Apparently, they must have targets set by these agencies to do outreach to women and minorities. That was really bad advice for us, since it distracted us from our core customers. Government work is just like private sector work – you need contacts and experience to get the work. For every person I know that got a government contract, I know a thousand more that wasted their time. I have to say that being certified has not been a tremendous benefit to us, and we have not received any work because we had the certification. That said, when companies look to cut firms, it has helped that we were one of the few MBE/WBE companies that they were using.

NUGGET #48 PR Is a Must!

By Sandi

You've heard it before and you'll hear it again. There is nothing like public relations. There is nothing like it if it's great, and there is most definitely nothing like it if it strips you of everything you have. Thankfully, Consultants 2 Go has not had the latter problem.

Our first award came from the New Jersey Association of Women Business Owners (NJAWBO). Peggy became a member the previous year, and we started to work closely with them. First, we won a bid to work on the strategy for The Women's Business Center. Peg got increasingly more involved and served on the board. That year, we doubled the revenues for our business and NJAWBO honored us with the Entrepreneur Achievement Award. With this came PR! Our pictures were published in newsletters, the Newark Star Ledger ran a small but well-viewed article on our company, and that gave us a much-needed credibility with potential clients. Out of the blue, people wanted to work with us.

At that point, we decided we were on to something. Some awards are bestowed on you, while others have very extensive and lengthy application processes. Winning the Make Mine a Million $ Business package came with a lot of potential PR at a much higher level than we were capable of soliciting ourselves. When we won, our company's name was splashed in major newspapers, magazines sought us out to write articles about us, and quite frankly, there were not a lot of organizations that were being backed at that level by major corporations whose expertise was marketing. At present, we still maintain a strong relationship with the Make Mine a Million $ Business team, and they still refer us when there is a PR opportunity that fits.

We also knew that writing articles was another way of getting our names in the right places. We wrote an article for American Banker that helped to establish us as experts in the bill payment industry. I can't say that we received any business from it, but what I can say is that when we were doing a presentation, handing out that article with our name on it afterwards certainly seemed to sway the vote towards us. Since that time, we have written articles on topics such as networking. We picked topics that we know from experience so that it rings true to our audience, and that give us the best PR of all, which is a referral or just word-of-mouth discussions with potential clients.

Good PR also came from the National Association of Women Business Owner's Promise Award. This award is given every year to an emerging businesswoman who has made an impact on the business world within five years and who shows great promise of becoming a Lifetime Achievement award winner (30+ years). We were on the local and national websites, in press releases and attended the gala dinner.

We have not yet gotten into blogging. I did set up a page but if you visit it, there will be nothing there. (Perhaps this is a cry for help?) It is an area which Consultants 2 Go is slowly beginning to learn and a late arrival to this area. What we have seen blogging do for clients is to ensure that they have a voice, and there are people who become "fans" who "follow" them and read their blog every single day. An email alert can be sent when an entry is made. This type of PR is priceless because the blogger is seen as an expert in a particular field, and becomes the "go-to" person for that industry.

The thing with PR is that most of the time we don't get to proofread and approve the article. So we don't know what will wind up being printed. We see it at the same time the rest of the world sees it. We have received misquotes, twisting of information and names left out where it was critical, and sometimes names left in where it should not have been. Some of that could have resulted in very bad press if our client became disgruntled about using their names in an article without permission.

Peggy: PR is about being accessible. If a reporter calls you for a story, chances are they are on deadline. You need to respond to them quickly if you want to be interviewed. They will not wait, so this means you have to drop everything to take their call. If you get the press, it can be well worth it. The same goes for the awards we apply for. They have deadlines, and sometimes they require a couple of hours of work. But putting in the time can really pay off with recognition from the press. We have seen the power of the press firsthand. And once the reporters know you, they will call you for future stories if they like you.

NUGGET #49 The Cobbler's Children Have No Shoes

By Sandi

We are the quintessential marketing company – website not up to date, finally got a nice brochure because the old trifold had poor quality paper and graphics, we don't pay for advertising or marketing – we go for the free stuff. We don't attend many trade shows – we wait to be comped by clients and we take forever to update our business and marketing plans.

That is because, as with all small companies, it is more profitable to spend our time working on other people's projects and making sure the marketing campaigns on which we work are perfect. Marketing our own company takes a back seat to the client's. Lately, we have made a concerted effort to come up to speed with our literature.

As part of a PR campaign, we hired a graphic artist and copywriter to work on our larger brochure. We had a small trifold brochure, and the content is still good today; however, visually, it is not representative of the type of work we do. As for marketing, our profit margin is tight, and it is difficult to scope out a definite budget. We do determine our budget by quarter or by what we need to do. We did spend approximately $10K on a fantastic PR campaign. It was extremely successful, giving us articles in magazines, being a guest on national radio shows, and a television appearance.

Our current trade strategy is to attend the trade shows and not participate as an exhibitor. We have tried exhibiting but our service is really not conducive to having a table. We do better when we walk around and speak to the people who are exhibiting since they are our potential clients.

We stop on a quarterly basis and assess our business strategy. We want to ensure we are doing for others what we should be doing for ourselves. It is important that we decide what marketing needs to be done in our business. We have opted to use low-cost avenues such as Constant Contact and social media like Linked In to keep our names in front of potential clients. Now, the cobbler's children have one shoe!

Peggy: Don't shortchange your business. Make sure you take the time to treat it like one of your best customers.

NUGGET #50 Workshops, Training Sessions and Coaches: Buyer Beware!

By Peggy

I am a big believer in continuous education for small business owners, and I attend as many workshops and classes to keep my skills current and my mind open. There are many free and low-cost training courses out there that are targeted at the small business owner, which are excellent. However, there are many more that charge high fees and are not much different in content than some of the courses or training that can be received for free or at reduced rates. I advise all business owners and would-be entrepreneurs to do some homework. Verify references and really understand the content before writing the check or spending the money.

Unfortunately, there are a lot of people out there who prey on the would-be or new entrepreneur. They offer fancy workshops and coaching with very little practical application or real life experience. I am very skeptical! Coaches can be wonderful if you choose the right one but, unfortunately it does not require a license or any certification to be a coach. Anyone can claim to be a coach. There are some organizations that provide certifications and training, so do your research and check their references. As part of Make Mine a Million $ Business, coaching was provided to us, and we had the chance to select from a choice of three coaches. Some coaches are individuals so you don't get a choice.

With the economy in a slump, there are a whole new crop of these people offering their services. Many want to practice on us, and we are their first guinea pigs. So beware. If only soft skills and empowerment are offered and they speak mainly about new-age principles without the practical know-how to go with it, I am suspicious. We need both to survive and thrive as a business. Women are especially targeted by and susceptible to these schemes. Perhaps some of these topics appeal to us more. I am not debating the need to believe in ourselves or some of these beliefs; in fact, I think it is crucial to success. However, we also need to know how to make sales calls, handle finances, negotiate contracts, secure insurance, and structure our businesses. And somehow, pretenders tend to shy away from these hard-core business topics. So please do your homework!

Sandi: Wow! The wound is still raw! There are coaches who give practical business advice, ones that give spiritual, personal guidance with action items and then there are the ones we disparagingly call "touchy-feely." There are coaches who:

a. Listen only – "we are not here to give you advice but to listen to you so that you can make your own decisions." If I'm paying you, I want expertise.

b. Tell you to "put it out there, speak it, claim it and the world will give it to you through good karma." Peggy and I would like to know *why*! If you say to me that people will not know what I need if I don't tell them, I can understand that. But we can't just drink the Koolaid: Peggy and Annette just paid $1,000 that we didn't have, to attend a sales coaching seminar that turned out to be a 2-day pitch for business from the presenter for her other workshops.

People learn in different ways. Some like the softer touch. We don't.

NUGGET #51 Social Media – Never Too Late to Learn

By Sandi

I don't understand it, but I had no choice but to learn about it and use it. Social media is the newest wave of marketing. I can't say that it's a fad because it's been around for a few years now and is being used by presidents to win campaigns. I was a late bloomer to this marketing idea. When I started to get "invites," I had no idea of what to do with them. Why were people sending me an email to read another email? Why do I need to log into a website or portal to pick up my information? I thought this was a big nuisance and for kids – I was too old for this.

When I finally ventured onto MySpace, mainly because I wanted to watch what the teenagers were up to, it was fairly simple, and I associated it with posting videos. The problem is I didn't have a video camera, and I had an old phone so who was going to actually take the videos for me to post? But as a marketing person, I understood the value of a "shared" server that everyone could see, especially the grandparents.

LinkedIn was next on my list for business purposes. It started to really take off at the time that I was displaced, so I put up a profile so that I could connect to other people. Once I started the business, it was a great way to find out consultants from particular companies. I had to learn how to use these tools in my own marketing of my business. And I was a resistor.

I quickly got the hang of Facebook because that seemed like a site to post pictures instead of videos. But I really did not want the entire world to see my pictures. And what about pictures of children? Do I post them? I had much reservation about Facebook but started to get "fans" and started to write on people's walls. Out of nowhere, people that I went to grad school with contacted me because they could now find me and keep in touch.

Just as I was getting the hang of Facebook, I understood that I needed to tweet. So, finally, I decided I needed to go to a bootcamp of some kind; otherwise, we would be left behind in the very new digital age of marketing and social media. I found and attended seminars with names like "The Glitter in Twitter." I had to quickly get an open mind to this new way of marketing. This is another instance of us being a marketing company but too busy (and stubborn) to learn new marketing techniques.

As I slowly put up my weekly tweet, I am becoming more comfortable with it and can barely remember why I was so resistant. Whether it is Twitter, Facebook, LinkedIn or any other forms of social media, I'm much more willing to get on board and learn. If I dislike them so much, perhaps I should start my own. In the meantime, follow me, friend me, fan me @sandiwebster…whatever! I might be sitting next to you in the next social media class and may just have something that will be new to you.

Peggy: I have to admit, Sandi was the first to get started with social media. I definitely started slowly, but now I am really hooked. There is tremendous power in social media and it can be a boon to small businesses, providing a dialogue with colleagues, clients, and prospects. I now have a column/blog, called Biz Buzz NJ, published in a digital newspaper, The Alternative Press, which I link to all my sites on Twitter, Facebook and LinkedIn. I am using some apps so that I can make one update and hit all the sites at once. I started with Tweet Deck but have just begun using Ping.fm to do this more effortlessly. I believe this is a whole new world, much like the internet in the 1990s and we have only begun to tap into its power. Look for me @peggymchale. Happy Tweeting!

The Golden Nugget

Quitters never win and winners never quit...especially successful business owners! (With apologies to Vince Lombardi and Napoleon Hill.) Starting and running a business will be one of the greatest challenges of your life so you will need to stay the course, be focused and never lose sight of your dream. Yes, you will be tested and it will be tough, but if you don't give up, you can make your dream a reality and hopefully get the gold too!

I hope we have inspired you to take the leap of faith and start and grow your business with blinders off. We wanted to share our journey with you since we had so many "a-ha" moments along the way. While we had read a lot of books on the topic, all seemed to miss the "eyewitness" account from the trenches that we thought was so important to share with others. These nuggets are things we learned while we were creating and growing our business. We always wished that someone had shared this with us at the beginning as it would have saved us some pain, money and time. Hopefully, we can help you by spreading our knowledge as you take your leap. Good luck!

About the Authors

Sandi Webster

is one of the principals of Consultants 2 Go, a marketing company that provides consultants to Fortune 500 corporations and mid-size companies. As such, she has spent years advising clients on the latest trends and strategies in marketing. She has over 20 years of experience and has managed all facets of new product launches, created and executed national direct mail campaigns, website launches and telemarketing programs. Her career spans American Express, Saks Fifth Avenue and the NYC Board of Education.

She holds an MBA in Marketing and belongs to organizations including National Association of Women Business Owners, National Association for Female Executives and the Manhattan Chamber of Commerce.

Peggy McHale,

also a principal of Consultants 2 Go, is a marketing guru acquiring her extensive senior management experience starting in telecommunications at AT&T, and ending an impressive corporate career as a vice president at American Express. She has developed marketing campaigns with wireless companies, credit card issuers, banks, insurance firms, and deregulated energy companies. Currently, Peggy is focused on building Consultants 2 Go into a noteworthy company that provides experienced, affordable marketing consultants. She has an MBA in finance and is a member of to the New Jersey Association of Women Business Owners, New Jersey Technology Council and Women's Presidents Organization. She is passionate about helping small business owners to grow their own businesses to the next level.